THE LIFE of JESUS

By Charles Hill

__JOHN 21:25__ - "And there are also many other things which Jesus did, the which, if they should be written every one, I suppose that even the world itself could not contain the books that should be written. Amen."

TABLE of CONTENTS

INTRODUCTION

Please do not read this book. It is not a novel or a fictional story. If you just read through it. You will miss the main subject of this book; Jesus. It is to be read carefully and prayerfully, studied that you may learn more about who and what Jesus is. I've spent many hours researching, and rechecking the facts so the information contained here is accurate.

On the inside cover of this book you read the following verse of scripture. This is the key verse for this book.

JOHN 21:25 - "And there are also many other things which Jesus did, the which, if they should be written every one, I suppose that even the world itself could not contain the books that should be written. Amen."

Jesus was the most influential person ever to have lived here on Earth. If you have a problem believing that, just look at the year on a calendar. That year is considered to be AD (*after death*). If that doesn't convince you, look at any legal document, it will say "In the year of our Lord." Having all of known time being based on the year of your birth is more than quite compelling! Think of this, whatever year it might have been before Jesus was born as a baby, automatically became BC (Before Christ).

The only way to truly know Jesus, is to have a personal relationship with Him. We must come to Him in faith believing that He is the son of God (*Hebrews 11:6 - "But without faith it is impossible to please Him: for he that cometh to God must believe that He is"*). How does this faith come? Romans 10:17 tells us: "So then faith cometh by hearing, and hearing by the word of God." For most of us, we were introduced to Jesus while someone spoke to us about Him, either in person (*Romans 10:14: " How then shall they call on Him in whom they have not believed? and how shall they believe in Him of whom they have not heard? and how shall they hear without a preacher?"*), or on some other form of media. However a large number of people have come to Him through reading the Bible. The Bible is the word of God!

While reading through the Gospels (*Matthew, Mark, Luke, John*) in the Bible; we see differences, some may call contradictions. I want to make it clear right now; there are no contradictions in the Bible! It is a simple case of not reading the whole Bible. This is why there are so many churches with different beliefs today. They will take a portion of scripture and base their doctrines on just one or two verses.

The purpose of this book is to hopefully eliminate this problem. We have to understand that the Gospel writers. Though they were inspired by God (*2 Timothy 3:16*), wrote from their own perspectives of what they saw. Think of a parade;

and you have four people standing on four different corners, watching the parade. After it is over, ask each person what they saw. If you haven't guessed, you'll get four different stories about the same parade. This is made evident by a chart found in the back of most Bibles called "Harmony of the Four Gospels." This is a list of stories from Matthew, Mark, Luke, and John. The chart lists the story and where it is found in each Gospel. The problem lies in that while John might have written about it. Mark doesn't mention it at all, and they may not even be the same story. A good example of this would be the thieves that were crucified with Jesus. Matthew tells us that both of the thieves were mocking Him (*Matthew 27:44*). While Luke tells us only one did (Luke 23:40-42). So, was it one or both? The answer is yes. I believe both thieves were what Matthew called "Mocking Him," <u>at first</u>. However, when Jesus made the statement "Father, forgive them; for they know not what they do" (*Luke 23:34*). One of them realized who or what Jesus was. In verse forty-two he called Jesus "Lord". You have to read all four to get the whole story. Remember, if we have difficulties with scripture, and if they are capable of rational intelligent explanations, then we do not have a contradiction. Since God cannot lie, then neither can His message to mankind be communicated by that which is a lie.

The four Gospel accounts differ from one another precisely because the authors had different audiences to whom they were addressing. Matthew was written for a Jewish audience. Mark was written mainly for Romans. Luke appears to be a personal letter to Theophilus. John writes to convince His readers that Jesus the Christ is actually the Son of God.

You will notice more than a few of the scriptures will reappear in two or more chapters. I believe this just goes to prove the continuity or consistency of the Word of God.

We always must keep in mind the key verse for this book; which is John 21:25: "And there are also <u>many other things which Jesus did</u>, the which, if they should be written every one, I suppose that even the world itself could not contain the books that should be written. Amen." I also need to include John 20:30 &31: "And many other signs truly did Jesus in the presence of His disciples, <u>which are not written in this book</u>: (V.31) But these are written, that ye might believe that Jesus is the Christ, the Son of God; and that believing ye might have life through His name." Jesus did so much that wasn't written down. We can speculate, but can't confirm on some subjects. So we have to take what the scriptures say (*as we should*) for the contents of this book.

You will also notice that I try to dispel false teaching, or beliefs on various subjects. I believe if we are going to learn, let's learn right.

You will notice most of the chapters are rather small. I'm not going into depths about doctrines and other subjects.   This book is as titled "The Life of Jesus." It's about His life, the people in His life, prophecy about His life, and much, much more.

LUKE 24:27 - *"And beginning at Moses and all the prophets, He expounded unto them in all the SCRIPTURES the things concerning Himself."*

WHY JESUS CAME

Have you ever wondered why God became a man, and came to earth to die for the sins of all mankind? It was love (*John 3:16*). Revelation 4:11 tells us that we were created for His pleasure. However, as sinful humans I doubt that we bring Him much pleasure. Romans 6:23a says "For the wages of sin is death," but then Ezekiel 33:11 says "I have no pleasure in the death of the wicked." So, a plan was made, even before the "foundation of the world," to come to us as a man to pay for our sins. This is where the end of Romans 6:23b comes into play "the gift of God is eternal life through Jesus Christ our Lord."

EPHESIANS 1:4 - "According as He hath

chosen us in Him (*Jesus*) before the foundation of the world, that we should be holy and without blame before Him in love."

<u>JOHN 3:16</u> - "For God so loved the world, that He gave His only begotten Son, that whosoever believeth in Him should not perish, but have everlasting life."

John three sixteen is probably the most well known verse in the Bible. However, most people can't quote the next two verses that come after it, and these are so very important.

<u>JOHN 3:17&18</u> - "For God sent not His Son into the world to condemn the world; but that the world through Him might be saved. (V.18) He that believeth on Him is not condemned: but he that believeth not is condemned already, because he hath not believed in the name of the only begotten Son of God."

So, what is this condemnation? Read the next two verses that come after that

<u>JOHN 3:19&20</u> - "And this is the condemnation, that light is come into the world, and men loved darkness rather than light, because their deeds were evil. (V.20) For every one that doeth evil hateth the light, neither cometh to the light, lest his deeds should be reproved."

God sent His Son into the world because He loves us, and all we have to do is believe it. He tells us that without Jesus in our life, we are condemned to die. But if we believe on Him we will be saved and not condemned.

As I stated above, God loves us. He has provided us a way to be with Him forever. This was accomplished through death and resurrection of His Son Jesus. In believing this we are not condemned. We are commended.

ROMANS 5:8-10 - "But God commendeth His love toward us, in that, while we were yet sinners, Christ died for us. (V.9) Much more then, being now justified by His blood, we shall be saved from wrath through Him. (V.10) For if, when we were enemies, we were reconciled to God by the death of His Son, much more, being reconciled, we shall be saved by His life.

Why did Jesus come? He had many reasons. Some of these are listed below.

MATTHEW 10:34 - "Think not that I am come to send peace on earth: I came not to send peace, but a sword."

MARK 2:17 - "When Jesus heard it, He saith unto them, They that are whole have no need of the physician, but they that are sick: I came not to call the righteous, but sinners to repentance."

LUKE 4:18&19 - "The Spirit of the Lord is upon me, because He hath anointed me to preach the gospel to the poor; He hath sent me to heal the brokenhearted, to preach deliverance to the captives, and recovering of sight to the blind, to set at liberty them that are bruised, (V.19) To preach the acceptable year of the Lord.

JOHN 6:38 - "For I came down from heaven, not to do mine own will, but the will of Him that sent me."

JOHN 12:47 - "And if any man hear my words, and believe not, I judge him not: for I came not to judge the world, but to save the world."

JOHN 16:28 - "I came forth from the Father, and am come into the world: again, I leave the world, and go to the Father."

JESUS AND PROPHECY

What is prophecy? According to the Greek word "Propheteia," the definition is: "A discourse emanating from divine inspiration and declaring the purposes of God, whether by reproving and admonishing the wicked, or comforting the afflicted, or revealing things hidden; esp. by foretelling future events." Prophecy and prophets are not fortune tellers. They are divinely inspired by God. Probably the most well known seer Nostradamus was not a prophet. He was raised in church, however when he turned to the occult, an evil spirit may have given him certain, but limited power beyond most human abilities. A true prophet declares the purposes of God. In this chapter we will look at the purpose of God to send us Himself wrapped up in a human form (1Timothy 3:16 *"And without controversy great is the mystery of godliness: <u>God was manifest in the flesh</u>, justified in the Spirit, seen of angels, preached unto the Gentiles, believed on in the world, received up into glory."*).This was not something He did in secret. He revealed His purpose to us through His prophets. In this chapter we will see what the prophets had to say about Jesus.

A PROPHETIC BIRTH

Matthew 1:22 - *"Now all this was done, that it might be fulfilled which was spoken of the Lord by the prophet, saying..."*

While reading through the four gospels, you will notice two reoccurring things Jesus made mention of. One was to do the will of His Father. The other was to make sure the prophecies concerning Him were fulfilled. There are over three hundred Messianic prophecies. The odds of Jesus fulfilling just forty eight of these would produce a number so large. The universe has no number that high.

In this section we will see that the birth of Jesus was planned long ago, right down to the very last detail. It was the fulfillment of many Old Testament prophecies. These prophecies were written between 1450 BC and 430 BC. That means they were written at least 400 to 1000 years before He was born.

It is said "the best place to start is at the beginning." That is exactly what we are going to do, considering the first verse we will look at is found in the book of Genesis. It is extremely important to remember Jesus was and is God in flesh (*Matthew 1:23*). John 1:1 tells us "In the beginning was the Word, and the Word was with God, and the Word was God." John 1:14 reveals to us that this "Word" was Jesus; "*And the Word was made flesh, and dwelt among us"* So, even though Jesus always was. He had to be born as a human to die for our sins. (*Romans 8:3 - "God sending his own Son in the likeness of sinful flesh, and for sin, condemned sin in the flesh."*) Remembering how John used the phrase "In the beginning." It did not seem odd to me; that Genesis, also started with the same exact words. Speaking of beginnings, let's go to Genesis where we find the first prophecies foretelling the birth of Jesus.

PROMISED THROUGH THE SEED OF ABRAHAM

MATTHEW 1:1 *-"The book of the generation of Jesus Christ, the son of David, the son of Abraham."*

Abraham:
GENESIS 22:18 - "And in thy (*Abraham*) seed shall all the nations of the earth be blessed; because thou hast obeyed my voice."

Isaac, the son of Abraham:
GENESIS 17:19 - "And God said, Sarah thy wife shall bear thee a son indeed; and thou shalt call his name Isaac: and I will establish my covenant with him for an everlasting covenant, and with his seed after him."

From tribe of Judah, The son of Isaac, which

was the son of Abraham:

GENESIS 49:10 - "The sceptre shall not depart from Judah, nor a lawgiver from between his feet, until Shiloh come; and unto him shall the gathering of the people be."

<u>HEIR TO THE THRONE OF DAVID</u>

ISAIAH 7:13&14 - "And he said, Hear ye now, O house of David; Is it a small thing for you to weary men, but will ye weary my God also?" (V.14) "Therefore the Lord Himself shall give you a sign; Behold, a virgin shall conceive, and bear a son, and shall call His name Immanuel." (*Matthew 1:23*)

ISAIAH 9:7 - "Of the increase of His government and peace there shall be no end, <u>upon the throne of David</u>, and upon His kingdom, to order it, and to establish it with judgment and with justice from henceforth even for ever. The zeal of the LORD of hosts will perform this."

ISAIAH 11:1 - "And there shall come forth a rod <u>out of the stem of Jesse</u> (*David's Father*), and a Branch shall grow out of his roots."

JEREMIAH 23:5 - "Behold, the days come, saith the LORD, that I <u>will raise unto David</u> a righteous Branch, and a King shall reign and prosper, and shall execute judgment and justice in the earth."

LUKE 1:31&33 - "And, behold, thou shalt conceive in thy womb, and bring forth a son, and shalt call His name JESUS. V.32 He shall be great, and shall be called the Son of the Highest: and the Lord God <u>shall give unto Him the throne of His father David</u>. (V.33)And He shall reign over the house of Jacob for ever; and of His kingdom there shall be no end."

LUKE 2:4 - "And Joseph also went up from Galilee, out of the city of Nazareth, into Judaea, unto the city of David, which is called Bethlehem; (because he was of the house and lineage of David:)"

Mary was a descendant of Solomon's brother Nathan who was born by Bathsheba making her part of the House of David.

JOHN 7:42 - "Hath not the scripture said, That <u>Christ cometh of the seed of David</u>, and out of the town of Bethlehem, where David was?"

The topic of this section is "A Prophetic Birth." Remembering that the word "prophecy" means to foretell. The verses ahead are literally a "who's who" of Major and Minor Prophets, that prophesied <u>specific</u> details concerning the coming Messiah. Listed first is the actual event from the New Testament, with its foretelling from the Old

Testament below each event.

<u>PLACE OF BIRTH</u>

<u>LUKE 2:4</u> - "And Joseph also went up from Galilee, out of the city of Nazareth, into Judaea, unto the city of David, which is called <u>Bethlehem</u>; (because he was of the house and lineage of David:)"

<u>MICAH 5:2</u> -"But thou, <u>Bethlehem</u> (*City of David*) Ephratah, though thou be little among the thousands of Judah, yet out of thee shall he come forth unto me that is to be ruler in Israel; whose goings forth have been from of old, from everlasting."

<u>TIME OF BIRTH</u>

<u>LUKE 2:5&6</u> - "To be taxed with Mary his espoused wife, being great with child. (V.6) And so it was, that, while they were there, <u>the days were accomplished that she should be delivered</u>."

<u>DANIEL 9:25</u>- "Know therefore and understand, that from the going forth of the commandment to restore and to build Jerusalem unto <u>the Messiah the Prince shall be seven weeks, and threescore and two weeks</u>: the street shall be built again, and the wall, even in troublous times."

BORN OF A VIRGIN

LUKE 1:26&27 - "And in the sixth month the angel Gabriel was sent from God unto a city of Galilee, named Nazareth, (V.27) To <u>a virgin</u> espoused to a man whose name was Joseph, of the house of David; and the virgin's name was Mary."

MATTHEW 1:22&23 - "Now all this was done, that it might be fulfilled which was spoken of the Lord by the prophet, saying, (V.23) Behold, <u>a virgin shall be with child</u>, and shall bring forth a son, and they shall call his name Emmanuel, which being interpreted is, God with us."

ISAIAH 7:14 - "Therefore the Lord Himself shall give you a sign; Behold, <u>a virgin shall conceive</u>, and bear a son, and shall call his name Immanuel."

WORSHIPED BY SHEPHERDS

LUKE 2:8, 16-18 - "And there were in the same country <u>shepherds abiding in the field</u>, keeping watch over their flock by night. (V.16) And <u>they came with haste, and found Mary, and Joseph, and the babe lying in a manger</u>. (V.17) And when they had seen it, they made known abroad the saying which was told them concerning this child. (V.18) And all they that heard it wondered at those things which were <u>told them by the shepherds</u>."

<u>**PSALM 72:9**</u> - "They that dwell in the wilderness (*shepherds*) <u>shall bow before Him</u>. "

<u>NO WISE MEN AT MANGER / STAR</u>

One of the most beloved and well known Christmas songs is "We Three Kings."

This may come as a shock to you, but there were no wise men at the manger, shepherds, yes, kings, no. We will see the Bible doesn't say they were, so there is no contradiction here. But wait; doesn't every nativity scene have three kings (*Wise men*) in it? Yes, but they (*the Wise men*) didn't show up until later. Let's read the familiar scriptures, and see why this is.

<u>**MATTHEW 2:1&2, 7, 9, 10&11**</u> - "Now when Jesus was born in Bethlehem of Judaea in the days of Herod the king, behold, there came wise men (*magi*) from the east to Jerusalem, (V.2) -Saying, Where is he that is born King of the Jews? for we have seen <u>His star in the east</u>, and are come to worship Him. (V.7) -Then Herod, when he had privily called the <u>wise men</u>, inquired of them diligently what time the star appeared. (V.9) - When they had heard the king, they departed; and, lo, the star, which they saw in the east, went before them, till it came and stood over where the young child was." (*Luke 2:12b - The angel told the shepherds: "Ye shall find the babe wrapped in*

swaddling clothes, lying in a manger.")

(V.10 & 11) - "When they <u>saw the star</u>, they rejoiced with exceeding great joy. (V.11) And when they were <u>come into the house</u>, they saw the <u>young child</u> with Mary His mother, and fell down, and worshipped Him: and when they had opened their treasures, they presented unto Him gifts; gold, and frankincense, and myrrh."

Yes, wise men did come and worship Jesus, but at a house, not at a stable. We will see more of that in this following section.

Looking at the scripture we see a reoccurring item in this story of the wise men; the star. These men were more than likely astrologers who saw a new star in the sky. There was a Messianic prophecy about a star coming out of Jacob.

<u>NUMBERS 24:17</u> - "I shall see Him, but not now: I shall behold Him, but not nigh: there shall come a <u>Star out of Jacob</u>, and a Sceptre shall rise out of Israel."

In this book I use scripture from the King James Version Bible. However, I want to use a verse from the apocrypha found in the book of Tobit. Tobit was part of the original Christian canon, but the apocrypha is not included in most Bibles. That being said, you can take it or leave it. I just thought this was interesting.

<u>**Tobit 13:11**</u> - "A bright light will shine to all parts of the earth; many nations shall come to you from afar, And the inhabitants of all the limits of the earth, drawn to you by the name of the Lord God, Bearing in their hands their gifts for the King of heaven. Every generation shall give joyful praise in you, and shall call you the chosen one, through all ages forever."

Now back to "The Star." This question has to be asked; "What time the star appeared?" I have a question myself; where was this star while Mary was pregnant? It is never mentioned that a star in the sky was hovering over Mary while she carried Jesus in her womb. I believe the star appeared at the birth of Jesus; thus, making it impossible for the wise men to be at the stable in time to see Jesus lying in a manger. When the wise men arrived, and saw Jesus, the term "young child," not "babe" was used to describe Him. The kicker is found back in verse eleven. The scripture says "when they were come into the house;" not the stable, but the house!

<u>WORSHIPED AND PRESENTED GIFTS BY KINGS</u>
"... Bearing gifts we travel afar..."

As mentioned above, yes, kings did come and worship Jesus. I don't believe there were just three guys on camels. They had to have had servants, think of a caravan. There were three separate kinds of gifts they brought. This is where we get the idea of three from. It was prophesied they would come.

MATTHEW 2:11 - "They (*the wise men*) saw the young child with Mary His mother, and fell down, and worshipped Him: and when they had opened their treasures, they presented unto Him gifts; gold, and frankincense, and myrrh."

PSALM 72:10 - "The kings of Tarshish and of the isles shall bring presents: the kings of Sheba and Seba shall offer gifts."

FLIGHT TO EGYPT

Right after these same Wise men were "warned of God in a dream that they should not return to Herod, they departed into their own country another way (*Matthew 2:12*).An angel appeared to Joseph, and told him to "flee into Egypt."

He probably thought "We have to protect Jesus from Herod. Or maybe he was thinking "thank You God for sending this angel to warn me." However it happened, I do not believe he considered the thought "Oh yeah, we got to go to Egypt to fulfill the prophecy in Hosea."

MATTHEW 2:13 - "And when they (*the wise men*) were departed, behold, the angel of the Lord appeareth to Joseph in a dream, saying, Arise, and take the young child and his mother, and flee into

Egypt, and be thou there until I bring thee word: for Herod will seek the young child to destroy him."

HOSEA 11:1 - "When Israel was a child, then I loved Him, and called my son out of Egypt."

WEEPING FOR THE CHILDREN

MATTHEW 2:16 - "Then Herod, when he saw that he was mocked of the wise men, was exceeding wroth, and sent forth, and slew all the children that were in Bethlehem, and in all the coasts thereof, from two years old and under, according to the time which he had diligently inquired of the wise men."

JEREMIAH 31:15 - "Thus saith the LORD; A voice was heard in Ramah, lamentation, and bitter weeping; Rahel weeping for her children refused to be comforted for her children, because they were not."

A MESSENGER SENT BEFORE

Hundreds of years before Jesus was born. It was prophesied that someone would be born to "prepare the way" for Him. This was basically to tell others that He was coming.

MARK 1:2-3 - "As it is written in the prophets,

Behold, <u>I send my messenger</u> (*John the Baptist*) before thy face, which <u>shall prepare thy way before thee</u>. (V. 3) The voice of one crying in the wilderness, Prepare ye the way of the Lord, make His paths straight.

<u>MALACHI 3:1</u> - "Behold, <u>I will send my messenger</u>, and he <u>shall prepare the way before me</u>: and the Lord, whom ye seek, shall suddenly come to his temple, even the messenger of the covenant, whom ye delight in: behold, he shall come, saith the LORD of hosts."

These are the events leading up to the birth of Jesus in a nutshell:

<u>MATTHEW 1:18-25</u> - "Now the birth of Jesus Christ was on this wise: When as His mother Mary was espoused to Joseph, before they came together, she was found with child of the Holy Ghost. (V.19) Then Joseph her husband, being a just man, and not willing to make her a public example, was minded to put her away privily. (V.20) But while he thought on these things, behold, the angel of the Lord appeared unto him in a dream, saying, Joseph, thou son of David, fear not to take unto thee Mary thy wife: for that which is conceived in her is of the Holy Ghost. (V.21) And she shall bring forth a son, and thou shalt call His name JESUS: for He shall save His people from their sins. (V.22) Now all this was done, that it might be fulfilled which was spoken of the Lord by the prophet, saying, (V.23) Behold, a virgin shall be with child, and shall bring forth a son, and they shall call His name Emmanuel, which being interpreted is, God with us. (V.24) Then Joseph being raised from sleep did as the angel of the Lord had bidden him, and took unto him his wife: (V.25) And knew her not till she had brought forth her firstborn son: and he called his name JESUS.

<u>A PROPHETIC LIFE</u>

I've already listed many of the prophecies related to Jesus' life here on earth. The majority of the prophecies concerning Jesus are related to His birth, which we have just seen; and to His death, which is to come. However, since the title of this book is "The Life of Jesus," I have to include the prophecies about the life of Jesus. Without including them all, I've chosen a few select ones I'd like to look at.

<u>HIS THRONE WILL BE ETERNAL</u>

<u>PSALM 45:6</u> - "Thy throne, O God, is <u>for ever and ever</u>: the sceptre of thy kingdom is a right sceptre."

<u>LUKE 1:31-33</u> - "And, behold, thou shalt conceive in thy womb, and bring forth a son, and shalt call His name JESUS. (V.32) He shall be great, and shall be called the Son of the Highest: and the Lord God shall give unto Him the throne of His father David: (V.33) And He shall reign over the house of Jacob for ever; and <u>of His kingdom there shall be no end</u>."

<u>HE WOULD BE A PRIEST AFTER THE ORDER OF MELCHIZEDEK</u>

Note: Melchizedek is not Jesus. In every reference, Jesus is said to be " after the order of Melchizedek."

<u>PSALM 110:4</u> - "The LORD hath sworn, and will not repent, Thou art a priest for ever <u>after the order of Melchizedek</u>."

<u>HEBREWS 5:5 &6</u> - "So also Christ glorified not Himself to be made an high priest; but He that said unto Him, Thou art my Son, to day have I begotten thee. (V.6) As He saith also in another place, Thou art a priest for ever <u>after the order of Melchisedec</u>."

<u>HE WILL SPEAK IN PARABLES</u>

<u>PSALM 78:2&3</u> - "I will open <u>my mouth in a parable</u>: I will utter dark sayings of old: (V.3) Which we have heard and known, and our fathers have told us."

MATTHEW 13:10 &11 - "And the disciples came, and said unto Him, Why speakest thou unto them in parables? (V.11) He answered and said unto them, Because it is given unto you to know the mysteries of the kingdom of heaven, but to them it is not given."

MATTHEW 13:34 &35 - "All these things spake Jesus unto the multitude in parables; and without a parable spake He not unto them: (V.35) That it might be fulfilled which was spoken by the prophet, saying, I will open my mouth in parables; I will utter things which have been kept secret from the foundation of the world."

HE WOULD BE SENT TO HEAL THE BROKENHEARTED

ISAIAH 61:1 - "The spirit of the Lord GOD is upon me; because the LORD hath anointed me to preach good tidings unto the meek; He hath sent me to bind up the brokenhearted, to proclaim liberty to the captives, and the opening of the prison to them that are bound; (V.2) To proclaim the acceptable year of the LORD, and the day of vengeance of our God; to comfort all that mourn."

LUKE 4:18 &19 - "The Spirit of the Lord is upon me, because He hath anointed me to preach the gospel to the poor; He hath sent me to heal the brokenhearted, to preach deliverance to the captives, and recovering of sight to the blind, to set at liberty them that are bruised, (V.19) To preach the acceptable year of the Lord."

<u>HE WOULD BE PRAISED BY LITTLE CHILDREN</u>

<u>PSALM 8:2</u> - "Out of <u>the mouth of babes and sucklings hast thou ordained strength</u> because of thine enemies, that thou mightest still the enemy and the avenger."

<u>MATTHEW 21:16</u> - "And said unto him, Hearest thou what these say? And Jesus saith unto them, Yea; have ye never read, <u>Out of the mouth of babes and sucklings thou hast perfected praise</u>?"

<u>A PROPHETIC DEATH</u>

As I mentioned before. There is a great amount of prophecy surrounding the death of Jesus.

An important aspect in the death of Jesus was that He HAD to be betrayed. Unfortunately it was one of His own chosen disciples who was to betray Him. Satan entered Judas Iscariot. He sold Jesus for thirty pieces of silver (*the price of a slave*), and finished the betrayal with a kiss.

<u>PSALM 41:9</u> - "Yea, <u>mine own familiar friend</u>, in whom I trusted, which did eat of my bread, hath lifted up his heel against me."

MATTHEW 26:14-16 - "Then one of the twelve, called Judas Iscariot, went unto the chief priests, (V.15) And said unto them, What will ye give me, and I will deliver Him unto you? And they covenanted with him for thirty pieces of silver. (V.16) And <u>from that time he sought opportunity to betray Him</u>."

LUKE 22:3 - "Then <u>entered Satan into Judas</u> surnamed Iscariot, being of the number of the twelve."

LUKE 22:47 - "And while He yet spake, behold a multitude, and he that was called Judas, one of the twelve, went before them, and drew near unto Jesus to kiss Him. (V.48) But Jesus said unto him, Judas, <u>betrayest thou the Son of man with a kiss</u>?"

When Judas saw what was happening to Jesus he must have had a change of heart. Many believe the reason he betrayed Jesus was to "push" Him into setting up his kingdom here. He may have had good intentions, but he was wrong.

MATTHEW 27:3&5 - "Then <u>Judas, which had betrayed Him</u>, when he saw that He was condemned, repented himself, and brought again the thirty pieces of silver to the chief priests and elders, (V.4) Saying, <u>I have sinned in that I have betrayed the innocent blood</u>. And they said, What is that to us? see thou to that. (V.5) And he cast down the pieces of silver in the temple, and departed, and went and hanged himself."

So, what did the chief priests do with the money? They unknowing fulfilled another prophecy!

MATTHEW 27:6-8 "And the chief priests took the silver pieces, and said, It is not lawful for to put them into the treasury, because it is the price of blood. (V.7) And they took counsel, and <u>bought with them the potter's field</u>, to bury strangers in. (V.8) Wherefore that field was called, The field of blood, unto this day."

ZECHARIAH 11:12 &13 "And I said unto them, If ye think good, give me my price; and if not, forbear. So they weighed for my price <u>thirty pieces of silver</u>. (V.13) And the LORD said unto me, <u>Cast it unto the potter</u>: a goodly price that I was prised (*valued*) at of them. And I took the thirty pieces of silver, and cast them to the potter in the house of the LORD."

At this point Jesus is taken to the house of the chief priest: (*Mark 14:53 "And they led Jesus away to the high priest: and with him were assembled all the chief priests and the elders and the scribes."* It was here that they held an illegal and unfair trial against Jesus. The following verses tell of some of the events that took place at this trial. *Note: From this point on you will see the prophecy followed by the fulfillment it.*

PSALM 35:11 - "<u>False witnesses</u> did rise up; they laid to my charge things that I knew not."

MARK 14:57 &58 - "And there arose certain, and bare <u>false witness</u> against him, saying, (V.58) We heard him say, I will destroy this temple that is made with hands, and within three days I will build another made without hands."

ISAIAH 53:7 - "He was oppressed, and He was afflicted, yet He opened not his mouth: He is brought as a lamb to the slaughter, and as a sheep before her shearers is dumb, so <u>He openeth not his mouth</u>."

MARK 15:4 &5 - "And Pilate asked him again, saying, <u>Answerest thou nothing</u>? behold how many things they witness against thee. (V.5) But <u>Jesus yet answered nothing</u>; so that Pilate marvelled."

ISAIAH 50:6 - "I gave my <u>back to the smiters,</u> and <u>my cheeks</u> to them that <u>plucked off the hair</u>: I hid not my face from <u>shame and spitting</u>."

MATTHEW 26:67 - "Then did they <u>spit</u> in His face, and <u>buffeted</u> Him; and others <u>smote</u> Him with the palms of their hands."

When the trial was over; Jesus was of course found guilty. Despite Pilates' attempts to save Him; Jesus was sentenced to be crucified. There were more than "quite a few" prophecies that came to pass on that hill called Calvary.

PSALM 22:16 - "For dogs have compassed me: the assembly of the wicked have enclosed me: they <u>pierced my hands and my feet</u>."
JOHN 20:25 - "The other disciples therefore said unto him, We have seen the Lord. But he said unto them, <u>Except I shall see in His hands the print of the nails, and put my finger into the print of the nails, and thrust my hand into His side</u>, I will not believe."

ISAIAH 53:12 - "Therefore will I divide him a portion with the great, and He shall divide the spoil with the strong; because He hath poured out his soul unto death: and <u>He was numbered with the transgressors</u>; and He bare the sin of many, and made intercession for the transgressors."
MATTHEW 27:38 - "Then were there two <u>thieves crucified with Him</u>, one on the right hand, and another on the left."

PSALM 69:21 - "They <u>gave me also gall</u> for my meat; and in my thirst they gave me <u>vinegar to drink</u>."
MATTHEW 27:34 - "They <u>gave Him vinegar to drink mingled with gall</u>: and when He had tasted thereof, He would not drink."

PSALM 109:4 - "For my love they are my

adversaries: but <u>I give myself unto prayer</u>."

LUKE 23:34 - "Then said Jesus, <u>Father, forgive them; for they know not what they do. And they parted His raiment, and cast lots</u>."

PSALM 22:18 - "They <u>part my garments</u> among them, and <u>cast lots</u> upon my vesture."

PSALM 22:7 &8 - "All they that see me <u>laugh me to scorn</u>: they shoot out the lip, they <u>shake the head</u>, saying, (V.8) <u>He trusted on the LORD that He would deliver Him: let Him deliver Him</u>, seeing He delighted in Him."

LUKE 23:35 - "And the people stood beholding. And the rulers also with them derided him, saying, He saved others; <u>let him save himself</u>, if he be Christ, the chosen of God."

MATTHEW 27:39 - "And they that passed by reviled Him, <u>wagging their heads</u>."

PSALM 22:1- "A Psalm of David. <u>My God, my God, why hast thou forsaken me</u>? why art thou so far from helping me, and from the words of my roaring?

MATTHEW 27:46 - "And about the ninth hour Jesus cried with a loud voice, saying, Eli, Eli, lama sabachthani? that is to say, <u>My God, my God, why hast thou forsaken me</u>?"

PSALM 34:20 - "He keepeth all his bones: <u>not one of them is broken</u>."

JOHN 19:32&33 - "Then came the soldiers,

and brake the legs of the first, and of the other which was crucified with Him. (V.33) But when they came to Jesus, and saw that He was dead already, <u>they brake not His legs</u>."

ZECHARIAH 12:10 - "And I will pour upon the house of David, and upon the inhabitants of Jerusalem, the spirit of grace and of supplications: and they shall look upon me <u>whom they have pierced</u>."
  JOHN 19:34 - "But one of the soldiers <u>with a spear pierced His side</u>, and forthwith came there out blood and water."

ISAIAH 53:9 - "And He made His grave with the wicked, and with <u>the rich in His death</u>; because He had done no violence, neither was any deceit in His mouth."
  MATTHEW 27:57&60 - "When the even was come, there came a <u>rich man</u> of Arimathaea, named Joseph, who also himself was Jesus' disciple (V. 60) <u>And laid it in his own new tomb</u>, which he had hewn out in the rock: and he rolled a great stone to the door of the sepulchre, and departed."

What a sad ending that would have been. However, that was not the end. Jesus told His disciples all this would happen to Him (*Mark 10:34: "And they shall <u>mock</u> Him, and shall <u>scourge</u> Him, and shall <u>spit</u> upon Him, and shall* *kill Him: and the third day He shall rise again.*"). He was in that tomb for three days; but He also came out of it alive! In Luke 24:5 we read that the angels who were at the tomb asked the women "Why seek ye the living among the dead?"

PSALM 16:10- "For thou wilt not leave my soul in hell; neither wilt thou suffer thine Holy One to see corruption.

PSALM 49:15- "But God will redeem my soul from the power of the grave: for He shall receive me. Selah.

MATTHEW 28:1-6- "In the end of the sabbath, as it began to dawn toward the first day of the week, came Mary Magdalene and the other Mary to see the sepulchre. (V.2) And, behold, there was a great earthquake: for the angel of the Lord descended from heaven, and came and rolled back the stone from the door, and sat upon it. (V.3) His countenance was like lightning, and his raiment white as snow: (V.4) And for fear of him the keepers did shake, and became as dead men. (V.5) And the angel answered and said unto the women, Fear not ye: for I know that ye seek Jesus, which was crucified. (V.6) He is not here: for He is risen, as He said*. Come, see the place where the Lord lay.

***MATTHEW 16:21**-"From that time forth

began Jesus to show unto His disciples, how that He must go unto Jerusalem, and suffer many things of the elders and chief priests and scribes, and be killed, and <u>be raised again the third day</u>."

It takes knowing dates which we won't go into here; but we know from the Bible that Jesus ascended back to heaven nine (*some say ten*) days before Pentecost and that He was crucified during the Passover. So, that would mean He was on earth approximately 40 days before He ascended to heaven. Luke tells us this in Acts,.

<u>**ACTS 1:2 &3**</u> - "Until the day in which He was taken up, after that He through the Holy Ghost had given commandments unto the apostles whom He had chosen: (V.3) To whom also He showed Himself alive after His passion by many infallible proofs, being <u>seen of them forty days</u>, and speaking of the things pertaining to the kingdom of God."

We have come to the end of the prophecies concerning Christ's earthly existence in His first coming. He had gone back home. John put it best in 3:13- "And no man hath ascended up to heaven, but He that came down from heaven, even the Son of man which is in heaven."

<u>**PSALM 24:7&8**</u> - "<u>Lift up your heads</u>, O ye gates; and be ye lift up, ye everlasting doors; and

the King of glory <u>shall come in</u>. (V.8) Who is this King of glory? The LORD strong and mighty, the LORD mighty in battle."

<u>MARK 16:19</u> - "So then after the Lord had spoken unto them, <u>He was received up into heaven</u>, and sat on the right hand of God."

<u>ACTS 1:9</u> - "And when He had spoken these things, while they beheld, <u>He was taken up; and a cloud received him out of their sight</u>."

Isaiah was a Old Testament prophet. So, obviously God had given him the gift of prophecy. In the fifty-third chapter of his book; Isaiah received detailed insight into the suffering of Jesus Christ as the Messiah. You will see some verses repeated from above. But, I wanted to include this section in complete context. I know this is all about Jesus. However, as I read this, I can't help to think it was all about us!

<u>Isaiah 53:3-11</u>- "He is despised and rejected of men; a man of sorrows, and acquainted with grief: and <u>we</u> hid as it were <u>our</u> faces from Him; He was despised, and <u>we</u> esteemed Him not. (V.4) Surely He hath borne <u>our</u> griefs, and carried <u>our</u> sorrows: yet <u>we</u> did esteem Him stricken, smitten of God, and afflicted. (V.5) But He was wounded for our transgressions, He was bruised for <u>our</u> iniquities: the chastisement of <u>our</u> peace was upon Him; and with His stripes <u>we</u> are healed. (V.6) All <u>we</u> like sheep have gone astray; <u>we</u> have turned every one to <u>his own</u> way; and the LORD hath laid on Him the iniquity of <u>us all</u>. (V.7) He was oppressed, and He was afflicted, yet He opened not His mouth: He is brought as a lamb to the slaughter, and as a sheep before her shearers is dumb, so He openeth not His mouth. (V.8) He was taken from prison and from judgment: and who shall declare His generation? for He was cut off out of the land of the living: <u>for the transgression of my people</u> was He stricken. (V.9) And He made His grave with the wicked, and with the rich in His death; because He had done no violence, neither was any deceit in His mouth. (V.10) Yet it pleased the LORD to bruise Him; He hath put Him to grief: when thou shalt make His soul an offering for sin, He shall see His seed, He shall prolong his days, and the pleasure of the LORD shall prosper in His hand. (V.11) He shall see of the travail of his soul, and shall be satisfied: by His knowledge shall my righteous servant justify many; for He shall bear <u>their iniquities</u>.

I mentioned above that we have come to the end of the prophecies concerning Christ's earthly existence in His first coming. However, this is not the end of the prophecies concerning Jesus. We have His word that some day He will come and "catch away" (*rapture*) the church (*saved souls*) into the clouds. Then later come back to Earth in what is called His "Second Coming." These are the only two prophecies left to be fulfilled.

1 THESSALONIANS 4:13-17 - "But I would not have you to be ignorant, brethren, concerning them which are asleep, that ye sorrow not, even as others which have no hope. (V.14) For if we believe that Jesus died and rose again, even so them also which sleep in Jesus will God bring with him. (V.15) For this we say unto you by the word of the Lord, that we which are alive and remain unto the coming of the Lord shall not prevent them which are asleep. (V.16) For the Lord Himself shall descend from heaven with a shout, with the voice of the archangel, and with the trump of God: and the dead in Christ shall rise.(V.17) Then we which are alive and remain shall be caught up together with them in the clouds, to meet the Lord in the air: and so shall we ever be with the Lord."

MATTHEW 24:30 - "And then shall appear the sign of the Son of man in heaven: and then shall all the tribes of the earth mourn, and they shall see the Son of man coming in the clouds of heaven with power and great glory."

REVELATION 22:20 - "He (*Jesus*) which testifieth these things saith, Surely I come quickly. Amen. Even so, come, Lord Jesus."

THE LIFE OF JESUS

JOHN 5:39 - *"Search the scriptures; for in them ye think ye have eternal life: and they are they which testify of me."*

CALLED A NAZARENE

I'm sure that if you've read the New Testament. You probably have seen how Jesus was also called "Jesus of Nazareth." It is mentioned twelve times total in all four gospels. This term is only to signify where He came from, not what His name was. This also is true for the name of Jesus Christ. Christ is not His last name. It is also a title, meaning Messiah, the Son of God.

MATTHEW 2:22b&23 - "being warned of God in a dream, he (*Joseph*) turned aside into the parts of Galilee: (V.23) And he came and dwelt in a city called Nazareth: that it might be fulfilled which was spoken by the prophets, He shall be called a Nazarene."

For many people, this verse is a cause of trouble since the prophecy that the Messiah would be called a Nazarene is nowhere to be found written in the Old Testament. That's because it was a spoken prophecy, not a written one. Some prophecies were spoken and not written. Some others were not spoken but only written, while some others were both spoken and written.

As mentioned above, the fact that Jesus "shall be called a Nazarene" is because He was from the city of Nazareth. He could have also been called a Nazarite. Below is the description of what is required to be a Nazarene.

<u>NUMBERS 6:1-8</u> - "And the LORD spake unto Moses, saying, (V.2) Speak unto the children of Israel, and say unto them, When either man or woman shall separate themselves to vow a vow of a Nazarite, to separate themselves unto the LORD: (V.3) He shall separate himself from wine and strong drink, and shall drink no vinegar of wine, or vinegar of strong drink, neither shall he drink any liquor of grapes, nor eat moist grapes, or dried. (V.4) All the days of his separation shall he eat nothing that is made of the vine tree, from the kernels even to the husk. (V.5) All the days of the vow of his separation there shall no razor come upon his head: until the days be fulfilled, in the which he separateth himself unto the LORD, he shall be holy, and shall let the locks of the hair of his head grow. (V.6) All the days that he separateth himself unto the LORD he shall come at no dead body. (V.7) He shall not make himself unclean for his father, or for his mother, for his brother, or for his sister, when they die: because the consecration of his God is upon his head. (V.8) All the days of his separation he is holy unto the LORD."

This description could not be referring to Jesus. He drank wine. He touched lepers and dead bodies too. The people of Nazareth were referred to as Nazarenes. It wasn't an accident Jesus came from Nazareth; it was to fulfill yet another prophecy.

<u>JOHN THE BAPTIST</u>

John the Baptist played a profound and prophetic role in the life of Jesus. Interestingly enough is the fact John and Jesus were related. When the angel Gabriel told Mary she would have a child (*even though she was a virgin*). He also told her that her cousin Elisabeth also conceived a son in her old age (*Luke 1:36*).

Being that they were related, naturally their children would be related also. To get a better idea of who and what John was. We need to look at chapter one in the book of Luke. Zacharias (*Johns' father*) was a priest going about his duties. When the angel Gabriel appeared to him. Gabriel told him that he and Elisabeth would have a son. Then he told him more than Zacharias could have imagined. They were to call his name John. He will be great in the sight of the Lord. He will be a Nazarene (even though they were from Judah); and because of him many of the children of Israel shall he turn to the Lord their God. There are three more things he said that I feel to be of extreme importance. Gabriel said that John "shall be filled with the Holy Ghost, even from his mother's womb." This would make John to be the first person in the Bible to be filled with the Holy Ghost. Up to this point in time the Holy Spirit had only come upon people. The second thing was, he said was "he shall go before Him in the spirit and power of Elias." There are some circles which preach that John the Baptist was Elijah come back down from heaven. This says in the spirit of Elias (*Elijah*).He was not Elijah! The third and last is the prophecy of Isaiah concerning "The voice of him that crieth in the wilderness." Of course he didn't name Zacharias son John to be that voice. Gabriel however did; the last thing he told Zacharias concerning John was that his ministry is "to make ready a people prepared for the Lord." John knew it too.

ISAIAH 40:3-5 - "The voice of him that crieth in the wilderness, Prepare ye the way of the LORD, make straight in the desert a highway for our God. (V.4) Every valley shall be exalted, and every mountain and hill shall be made low: and the crooked shall be made straight, and the rough places plain: (V.5) And the glory of the LORD shall be revealed, and all flesh shall see it together: for the mouth of the LORD hath spoken it."

LUKE 3:3-6 - "And he (*John*) came into all the country about Jordan, preaching the baptism of repentance for the remission of sins; (V.4) As it is written in the book of the words of Esaias the prophet, saying, The voice of one crying in the wilderness, Prepare ye the way of the Lord, make his paths straight. (V.5) Every valley shall be filled, and every mountain and hill shall be brought low; and the crooked shall be made straight, and the rough ways shall be made smooth; (V.6) And all flesh shall see the salvation of God."

If you still are wondering; what importance does John the Baptist have in the life of Jesus? The bottom line is; more than anything else, there was a Messianic prophecy that had to be fulfilled. God chose to bless Zacharias and Elisabeth with a child that would be the fulfillment of the prophecy. This fulfillment was of extreme importance to prove Jesus was indeed the Messiah. Let's look at the Baptism of Jesus.

<u>THE BAPTISMS OF JESUS</u>

Why was Jesus baptized? Was the baptism of Jesus important? At first glance, it seems that Jesus' baptism has no purpose at all. John's baptism was the baptism of repentance (*Matthew 3:11*), but Jesus was sinless and had no need of repentance. Even John questioned Jesus' coming to him. John recognized his own sin and was aware that he, a sinful man in need of repentance himself, was unfit to baptize the spotless Lamb of God.

(*The objection that John made against baptizing Jesus bears resemblance to what Peter did, when Jesus went to wash his feet*). However, Jesus told him that it should be done because it was us "to fulfill all righteousness."

<u>MATTHEW 3:14&15</u> - "But John forbad Him, saying, I have need to be baptized of thee, and comest thou to me? (V.15) And Jesus answering said unto him, Suffer (*permit*) it to be so now: for thus it becometh us to fulfil all righteousness. Then he suffered Him."

There are several reasons why it was fitting for John to baptize Jesus at the beginning of Jesus' public ministry. Jesus was about to embark on His great work, and it was appropriate that He be recognized publicly by His forerunner. John was the "voice crying in the wilderness" prophesied by Isaiah, calling people to repentance in preparation for their Messiah.

<u>ISAIAH 40:3</u> - "The voice of him that crieth in the wilderness, Prepare ye the way of the LORD, make straight in the desert a highway for our God."

By baptizing Him, John was declaring to all that here was the One they had been waiting for, the Son of God, the One he had predicted would baptize "with the Holy Ghost and fire." This is the fulfilling of all righteousness mentioned earlier.

<u>**MATTHEW 3:11**</u> - "I indeed baptize you with water unto repentance: but He that cometh after me is mightier than I, whose shoes I am not worthy to bear: He shall baptize you with the Holy Ghost, and with fire."

Jesus' baptism by John takes on added interest when we consider that John was of the tribe of Levi and a direct descendant of Aaron. Luke specifies that both of John's parents were of the Aaronic priestly line (*Luke 1:5*). One of the duties of the priests in the Old Testament was to present the sacrifices before the Lord. John the Baptist's baptism of Jesus could be seen as a priestly presentation of the Ultimate Sacrifice. John's words the day after the baptism have a decidedly priestly air: "Behold the Lamb of God, which taketh away the sin of the world!"

<u>**JOHN 1:29**</u> - "The next day John seeth Jesus coming unto him, and saith, Behold the Lamb of God, which taketh away the sin of the world."

Perhaps most importantly; was the occasion for them and all future generations to see the perfect embodiment of the triune God revealed on that day. They received a testimony directly from heaven of the Father's pleasure with the Son, and the descending of the Holy Spirit upon Jesus.

MATTHEW 3:16&17 - "And Jesus, when He was baptized, went up straightway out of the water: and, lo, the heavens were opened unto Him, and he saw the Spirit of God descending like a dove, and lighting upon Him: (V.17) And lo a voice from heaven, saying, This is my beloved Son, in whom I am well pleased."

Here is a little tidbit that is often overlooked. Matthew and Mark both said that Jesus came "straightway out of the water;" then the voice from heaven, and the appearing of the dove occurred. Luke is where the tidbit comes from. He lets us know that Jesus was praying when He was being baptized.

LUKE 3:21 - "Now when all the people were baptized, it came to pass, that Jesus also being baptized, and <u>praying</u>, the heaven was opened."

This topic has a lot more importance than what I first thought. I believed that Jesus was baptized, to show us we need to be baptized also. It was another one of those "He did it for us" moments. After all, baptism does not redeem us from our sins. We are baptized to show that we have been redeemed of our sins by the blood of Jesus.

COLOSSIANS 2:12 - "Buried with Him in

baptism, wherein also ye are risen with Him through the faith of the operation of God, who hath raised Him from the dead."

Interestingly enough, this is one of the events in the life of Jesus that all four of the gospel writers included. I've taken excerpts from each one, and pieced together a chronological order of the baptism of Jesus

MARK 1:1-4, 7&8 - "The beginning of the gospel of Jesus Christ, the Son of God; (V.2) As it is written in the prophets, Behold, I send my messenger before thy face, which shall prepare thy way before thee. (V.3) The voice of one crying in the wilderness, Prepare ye the way of the Lord, make his paths straight. (V.4) John did baptize in the wilderness, and preach the baptism of repentance for the remission of sins. (V.7) And preached, saying, There cometh one mightier than I after me, the latchet of whose shoes I am not worthy to stoop down and unloose. (V.8) I indeed have baptized you with water: but he shall baptize you with the Holy Ghost.

MATTHEW 3:13-17 - "Then cometh Jesus from Galilee to Jordan unto John, to be baptized of him. (V.14) But John forbad Him, saying, I have need to be baptized of thee, and comest thou to me? (V.15) And Jesus answering said unto him, Suffer it to be so now: for thus it becometh us to fulfil all righteousness. Then he suffered Him.

(V.16) And Jesus, when He was baptized, went up straightway out of the water: and, lo, the heavens were opened unto him, and he saw the Spirit of God descending like a dove, and lighting upon him: (Luke 3:22 "And the Holy Ghost descended in a bodily shape like a dove upon Him.") (V.17) And lo a voice from heaven, saying, This is my beloved Son, in whom I am well pleased.

John the Baptist had an important role in this particular baptism. Who knows how many people he had baptized before Jesus came to him? As I mentioned before that John was of the tribe of Levi and a direct descendant of Aaron. He had a unique relationship with God the Father. Luke 3:2b tells us that "the word of God came unto John the son of Zacharias in the wilderness." God would show Him what he was to do. Not only was John supposed to prepare the way for Jesus. He was supposed to baptize Him. Do you think the fact that "the Holy Ghost descended in a bodily shape like a dove upon Him" is of any other significance than to show the trinity of God? John was told to watch for this to happen. Then whoever it was that the Spirit descended upon, and remained on Him. This was the Messiah.

JOHN 1:30-34 - "This is He of whom I said, After me cometh a man which is preferred before me: for He was before me. (V.31) And I knew Him not: but that He should be made manifest to Israel, therefore am I come baptizing with water. (V.32) And John bare record, saying, I saw the Spirit descending from heaven like a dove, and it abode upon him. (V.33) And I knew Him not: but He that sent me to baptize with water, the same said unto me, Upon whom thou shalt see the Spirit descending, and remaining on Him, the same is He which baptizeth with the Holy Ghost. (V.34) And I saw, and bare record that this is the Son of God."

Was the baptism of Jesus important? You better believe it!

Jesus spoke of another baptism that He must go through (*endure is a better word*). This one had nothing to do with water.

In Matthew 20:20 we are told "Then came to Him (*Mary*) the mother of Zebedee's children with her sons, worshipping Him, and desiring a certain thing of Him. The request was to "Grant that these my two sons (*James and John*) may sit, the one on thy right hand, and the other on the left, in thy kingdom." Jesus told her "Ye know not what ye ask." Then He said something they totally misunderstood.

MARK 10:38&39 - "But Jesus said unto them, Ye know not what ye ask: can ye drink of the cup that I drink of? and be baptized with the baptism that I am baptized with? (V.39) And they said unto Him, We can. And Jesus said unto them, Ye shall indeed drink of the cup that I drink of; and with the baptism that I am baptized withal shall ye be baptized."

Jesus was using the words cup" and "baptized" to refer to what awaited Him in Jerusalem. The cup is a cup of suffering and pain which Jesus will drink. Jesus' prayer to be spared the cup if it is God's will makes the cup stand for all the suffering of the cross He will endure. In the OT, the word for "cup" is used metaphorically to refer to divine wrath or punishment in response to sin and rebellion. The baptism of Jesus here is full immersion in humiliation, degradation, pain, and suffering on an unimaginable scale. The use of "baptism" in parallel with "cup" indicates that it is also a metaphor for suffering. The two images together reinforce the suffering to come that Jesus will face and that his disciples will also eventually face. I've added these two verses that holds much weight.

LUKE 12:50 - "But I have a <u>baptism</u> to be baptized with; and how am I straitened (*to press on every side*) till it be accomplished!"

MATTHEW 26:42 -"He went away again the second time, and prayed, saying, O my Father, if this <u>cup</u> may not pass away from me, except I drink it, Thy will be done."

Jesus told them they would suffer the same

thing because of their stand for Him: "Ye shall indeed drink of the cup that I drink of; and with the baptism that I am baptized withal shall ye be baptized."

While wrapping up the study of Jesus' baptisms. I thought it was good to let you know that the Bible tells us that Jesus never baptized anyone.

JOHN 4:1&2 - "When therefore the Lord knew how the Pharisees had heard that Jesus made and baptized more disciples than John, (V.2) (Though Jesus himself baptized not, but his disciples.)"

It wasn't that He was against it. Soon He would be baptizing all kinds of people.

MARK 1:8 "I indeed have baptized you with water: but He shall baptize you with the Holy Ghost."

In fact He includes it in His farewell speech to His disciples.

MARK 16:15&16 - "And He said unto them, Go ye into all the world, and preach the gospel to every creature.(V.16) He that believeth <u>and is baptized</u> shall be saved; but he that believeth not shall be damned."

It is important to notice the last line in that

verse. It is not being baptizes that saves you. (Remember the thief on the cross). "he that <u>believeth not</u> shall be damned."

The Apostle Paul felt the same way:

<u>**1 CORINTHIANS 1:16&17**</u> - "And I baptized also the household of Stephanas: besides, I know not whether I baptized any other. (V.17) For Christ sent me not to baptize, but to preach the gospel: not with wisdom of words, lest the cross of Christ should be made of none effect."

<u>THE APOSTLES</u>

Here we have a topic the skeptics use to claim of a contradiction in the Bible. They say Matthew and Mark list of the apostles is the same group of people, but Luke's list is different. I'll be the first to admit it, yes, they are different. At one time I wondered about this myself. However, knowing there are no contradiction in the Bible. I set out to study this topic. My findings were; they are different, but the same. Let's look at the lists. Then, I will reveal why my results are as they are. (*John has no list*).

<u>**MATTHEW 10:2-4**</u> - "Simon, who is called Peter, and Andrew his brother; James the son of Zebedee, and John his brother; V.3 Philip, and Bartholomew; Thomas, and Matthew the publican;

James the son of Alphaeus, and Lebbaeus, whose surname was Thaddaeus; V.4 Simon the Canaanite, and Judas Iscariot, who also betrayed Him."

MARK 3:16-19 - "And Simon he surnamed Peter; (V.17) And James the son of Zebedee, and John the brother of James; (V.18) And Andrew, and Philip, and Bartholomew, and Matthew, and Thomas, and James the son of Alphaeus, and Thaddaeus, and Simon the Canaanite, (V.19) And Judas Iscariot, which also betrayed Him."

LUKE 6:14-16 - "Simon, (whom he also named Peter,) and Andrew his brother, James and John, Philip and Bartholomew, (V.15) Matthew and Thomas, James the son of Alphaeus, and Simon called Zelotes, (V.16) And Judas the brother of James, and Judas Iscariot, which also was the traitor."

When looking at the three gospels. You will find Matthew and Mark are exactly the same. However, it would appear that Luke had omitted Thaddaeus, and inserted the name of Judas the brother of James in its place. This is where the skeptics cry "contradiction!" The fact of the matter is that Thaddaeus, was also named Judas the brother of James. Luke who also wrote the book of Acts used this name again when listing the apostles who went into an upper room to hide; after the crucifixion of Jesus.

ACTS 1:13 - "And when they were come in, they went up into an upper room, where abode both Peter, and James, and John, and Andrew, Philip, and Thomas, Bartholomew, and Matthew, James the son of Alphaeus, and Simon Zelotes, and Judas the brother of James (*Thadeus*)."

You may be saying "yeah right, you're just reaching." It makes sense though. I suppose you've never heard of a nickname, an alias, or even using another name altogether? There is no reason Thaddaeus could not also be called Judas. Matthew referred to him in this manner, "Lebbaeus, whose surname was Thaddaeus." It is a practice that is ageless; here are some examples.

GENESIS 17:5 - "Neither shall thy name any more be called Abram, but thy name shall be Abraham."

MATTHEW 10:2 - "Simon, who is called Peter"

LUKE 6:15 - "Simon called Zelotes"

ACTS 1:23 - "Joseph called Barsabas, who was surnamed Justus"

ACTS 13:9 - "Then Saul, (who also is called

Paul,)"

ACTS 15:37 -"And Barnabas determined to take with them John, whose surname was Mark."

As I stated above. This topic is one of the skeptic's favorite arguments for a contradiction in the Bible. I really don't see what the big deal is. There had to be twelve apostles (*Luke 22:29&30 "And I appoint unto you a kingdom, as my Father hath appointed unto me; (V.30) That ye may eat and drink at my table in my kingdom, and sit on thrones judging the twelve tribes of Israel."*). Matthew, Mark, and Luke each had twelve names listed. It's not too far of a reach, to assume they were referring to the same twelve men.

Speaking of twelve; did you happen to notice the exclusion of one name in Luke's list of apostles in the upper room?

ACTS 1:13 - "And when they were come in, they went up into an upper room, where abode both Peter, and James, and John, and Andrew, Philip, and Thomas, Bartholomew, and Matthew, James the son of Alphaeus, and Simon Zelotes, and Judas the brother of James (Thadeus)."

The name of Judas Iscariot is not mentioned. Peter told the others "he was numbered with us, and had obtained part of this ministry" (*Acts 1:17*). They needed to find a replacement, so that there would be twelve again (*Luke 22:30*). This distinction fell on an unknown (*to us*) man named Matthias.

ACTS 1:26 - "And they gave forth their lots; and the lot fell upon Matthias; and he was numbered with the eleven apostles (*and never mentioned again*)."

It is a widely known fact among most Bible scholars; God wanted Paul to be the twelfth apostle. Eventually Paul did received his calling and this is an example of how he would start his letters to a church, "Paul, an apostle of Jesus Christ by the will of God" He wouldn't have called himself an apostle if he wasn't one.

1 CORINTHIANS 15:6-9 - "After that, He (*Jesus*) was seen of above five hundred brethren at once; of whom the greater part remain unto this present, but some are fallen asleep. (V.7) After that, He was seen of James; then of all the apostles. (V.8) And last of all He was seen of me also, as of one born out of due time. (V.9) For I am the least of the apostles, that am not meet to be called an apostle, because I persecuted the church of God."

THE TRANSFIGURATION

I find this event in the life of Jesus to be of particular interest. This was a onetime occurrence, never happened before, and was not repeated (*by anyone*). There is something about it that I find to baffling. This story is found in all the Gospels except Johns. I don't find that baffling. What I find baffling is that he was one of the chosen three that saw this, and didn't write a thing about such an awesome display he had experienced.

I am speaking about what is called "The Transfiguration of Jesus." I guess it is called this because of what Matthew wrote in this verse.

MATTHEW 17:2 - "And was transfigured before them: and His face did shine as the sun, and His raiment was white as the light."

I mentioned that you can find the recorded witnessing of this transfiguration in the books of Matthew, Mark and Luke. They all tell the same basic story. However Luke went into a little more depth than the others did, so we will use his account. (*I've underlined the extra details the others left out*).

LUKE 9:28- 36- "And it came to pass about an <u>eight</u> days after these sayings, He took Peter and John and James, and went up into a mountain <u>to pray</u>. (V.29) And as He prayed, the fashion of His countenance was altered, and His raiment was white and glistering. (V.30) And, behold, there talked with Him two men, which were Moses and Elias (Elijah): (V.31) Who appeared in glory, and spake <u>of His decease (death) which He should</u>

accomplish at Jerusalem.(V.32) But Peter and they that were with Him <u>were heavy with sleep</u>: and when they were awake, they saw His glory, and the two men that stood with Him. (V.33) And it came to pass, as they departed from Him, Peter said unto Jesus, Master, it is good for us to be here: and let us make three tabernacles; one for thee, and one for Moses, and one for Elias: not knowing what he said. (V.34) While he thus spake, there came a cloud, and overshadowed them: and they feared as they <u>entered into</u> the cloud. (V.35) And there came a voice out of the cloud, saying, This is my beloved Son: hear Him. (V.36) And when the voice was past, Jesus was found alone. And they kept it close, and told no man in those days any of those things which they had seen."

The story is pretty much self explanatory and doesn't need to be elaborated on. I would however like you to notice in verse thirty six, the phrase "and told no man in those days." Why didn't they tell anyone about such a great thing they had experienced? Also, what were "those days?" Once again, we have to read the other accounts of this story to find the answer.

<u>**MATTHEW 17:9**</u> - "And as they came down from the mountain, Jesus charged them, saying, Tell the vision to no man, until the Son of man be risen again from the dead."

<u>**MARK 9:9**</u> - "And as they came down from the mountain, He charged them that they should tell no man what things they had seen, till the Son of man were risen from the dead."

As I said, this story is pretty much self explanatory. That does not diminish its importance at all. How many people can say that they were changed, glowed, talked in person with Moses and Elijah, and had a voice come out of the cloud, saying, "This is my beloved Son (*in whom I am well pleased- Matthew 17:5*), hear Him," all in one afternoon? No one but Jesus can!

<u>REJECTION OF THE CORNERSTONE</u>

<u>*LUKE 17:25*</u> - *"But first must he suffer many things, and be rejected of this generation."*

Jesus knew He was going to be rejected not only by the people, but also by the elders and chief priests and scribes. Here He tells them this.

<u>**MATTHEW 21:42**</u> - "Jesus saith unto them, Did ye never read in the scriptures, The stone which the builders rejected, the same is become the head of the corner: this is the Lord's doing, and it is marvellous in our eyes?"

The verses Jesus was referring to was yet another prophecy:

<u>**PSALM 118:22&23**</u> - "The stone which the builders refused is become the head stone of the corner. V.23 This is the LORD'S doing; it is marvellous in our eyes."

If that particular passage wasn't enough proof for them. There were other verses they should have known concerning the Messiah; but they really didn't want to know.

<u>**ISAIAH 53:3**</u> - "He is despised and rejected of men; a man of sorrows, and acquainted with grief: and we hid as it were our faces from Him; He was despised, and we esteemed Him not."

<u>**PSALM 69:8**</u> - "I am become a stranger unto my brethren, and an alien unto my mother's children."

<u>New Testament:</u>
<u>**JOHN 1:11**</u> - "He came unto His own, and His own received Him not."

<u>WHY JESUS USED PARABLES</u>

The definition of a parable is "a short simple story intended to illustrate a moral or religious lesson." Jesus used parables to make His lessons easier for the people to understand. However, He had His reasons for using them too. The bottom line though is this was another way of fulfilling the prophecies about Him.

MATTHEW 13:3, 10&11 - "And <u>He spake many things unto them in parables</u>. (V.10) -And the disciples came, and said unto Him, Why speakest thou unto them in parables? (V.11) He answered and said unto them, Because it is given unto you to know the mysteries of the kingdom of heaven, but to them it is not given."

PSALM 78:2- "I will open my mouth in a parable: I will utter dark sayings of old."

MATTHEW 13:13&14 - "Therefore speak I to them in parables: because they seeing see not; and hearing they hear not, neither do they understand. (V.14) And in them is <u>fulfilled the prophecy</u> of Esaias, which saith, By hearing ye shall hear, and shall not understand; and seeing ye shall see, and shall not perceive." (*Isaiah 6:9 & 10*)

THE POWER OF JESUS

After Jesus was resurrected the eleven disciples went into Galilee, to a mountain place where Jesus had told them He'd be. He being in His glorified state told them this.

MATTHEW 28:18 - "And Jesus came and spake unto them, saying, **All** power is given unto me in heaven and in earth."

So, how much power is "all" power? I have done an extensive study on the word "all," and it means "all." There is no elaborate here.

We find that Jesus has all this power; but what happens when He gives some of this power away? Jesus gave His disciples power. Then He extended power to seventy others, and finally more to anyone who believes in Him.

MATTHEW 10:1 - "And when He had called unto Him His twelve disciples, He gave them power against unclean spirits, to cast them out, and to heal all manner of sickness and all manner of disease."

LUKE 10:19 - "Behold, I give unto you power to tread on serpents and scorpions, and over all the power of the enemy: and nothing shall by any means hurt you."

LUKE 10:1&17 - "After these things the Lord appointed other seventy also, and sent them two and two before His face into every city and place, whither He Himself would come. (V.17) And the seventy returned again with joy, saying, Lord, even the devils are subject unto us through thy name."

MARK 16:17&18 - "And these signs shall follow them that believe; In my name shall they cast out devils; they shall speak with new tongues; (V.18) They shall take up serpents; and if they drink any deadly thing, it shall not hurt them; they shall lay hands on the sick, and they shall recover."

With Jesus giving out all this power; does He still have "all" power? This question might be confusing to those who have read about "the woman with the issue of blood." Without getting into the whole story; when she pushed through the crowd and touched Him, Jesus said "power is gone out of me."

LUKE 8:46 - "And Jesus said, Somebody hath touched me: for I perceive that virtue (*power*) is gone out of me."

If power is gone from Him; does He still have "all" power. The answer is yes! Jesus speaks this here, not in a way of complaint, as if He were either weakened or wronged, but in a way of satisfaction. It was His delight that virtue (power) was gone out of Him to do someone good, and He did not grudge doing it. He had no less power in Him for the going out of the virtue from Him; for He is an overflowing fountain of power.

CASTING OUT EVIL SPIRITS

Jesus had the power, and authority over evil, and unclean spirits (*Luke 4:36*). Here we have the story of a man who called himself Legion, who had many devils.

In Matthew, read that there were two possessed with devils. However in Mark and Luke it is said to be one man possessed with an unclean spirit. If there were two, there was one, and Mark does not say that there was only one; so that this difference cannot give us any just question; it is probable that one of them was much more remarkable than the other, and said what was said. Some think, these two were man and wife, because the other Gospels speak of only one. I do not believe that is the case. It is funny, how this difference can be solved by the pigs in each story. In all three instances the devils asked to be cast into the swine. Then the whole herd of swine ran violently down a steep place into the sea, and perished in the waters. Clearly these are all the same stories.

MATTHEW 8:28 -"And when He was come to the other side into the country of the Gergesenes, there met Him <u>two possessed with devils</u>, coming out of the tombs, exceeding fierce, so that no man might pass by that way."

MATTHEW 8:31-"So the devils besought Him, saying, If thou cast us out, suffer us to go away into the herd of swine."

MARK 5:1& 2 - "And they came over unto the other side of the sea, into the country of the Gadarenes. (V.2) And when He was come out of the ship, immediately there met Him out of the tombs <u>a man</u> with an unclean spirit."

<u>MARK 5:11& 12</u> - "Now there was there nigh unto the mountains a great herd of swine feeding. (V.12) And all the devils besought Him, saying, Send us into the swine, that we may enter into them."

<u>LUKE 8:26& 27</u> - "And they arrived at the country of the Gadarenes, which is over against Galilee. V.27 And when He went forth to land, there met Him out of the city <u>a certain man</u>, which had devils long time, and ware no clothes, neither abode in any house, but in the tombs."

<u>LUKE 8:32</u> - "And there was there an herd of many swine feeding on the mountain: and they besought Him that He would suffer them to enter into them."

<u>FEEDING THE MULTITUDES</u>

Most people, who are familiar with stories from the Bible, have heard about the feeding of the five thousand. Some of these will say there are differences in the story, claiming a contradiction. Once again there are no contradictions, but there are two different stories. First Jesus fed five thousand (*actually more*), then He fed four thousand. The feeding of the five thousand appears in all four gospels. Matthew, Mark, and Luke all tell the same story down to the last detail.

<u>MATTHEW 14:17,20& 21</u> - "And they say unto Him, We have here but five loaves, and two fishes. (V.20) -And they did all eat, and were filled: and they took up of the fragments that remained twelve baskets full. (V.21) And they that had eaten were about five thousand men, beside women and children.

Only in John do we find where the five loaves, and two fish came from. Considering the numbers are the same in all four stories. These loaves and fish had to come from this unnamed "lad."

<u>JOHN 6:9</u> - "There is a lad here, which hath five barley loaves, and two small fishes: but what are they among so many?"

The story of the feeding of the four thousand is found only in Matthew and Mark.
This is where the people claiming a contradiction err. If they were aware that there were two separate instances of Jesus feeding a multitude. They would see why the differences occur. Matthew tells exactly same story as Mark.

<u>MARK 8:5,7-9</u> - "And He asked them, How many loaves have ye? And they said, <u>Seven</u>. (V.7) And they had <u>a few</u> small fishes: and He blessed, and commanded to set them also before them. (V.8) So they did eat, and were filled: and they took up of the broken meat that was left <u>seven</u> baskets. (V.9) And they that had eaten were about <u>four thousand</u>: and He sent them away."

So, there cannot be a contradiction when these are two separate events!

<u>MIRACLES OF JESUS</u>

I'm not going to spend a lot of time on this subject. You can find most of what is here in this and other chapters of this book. The gospels list at least thirty seven detailed miracles of Jesus. There are thirty nine if you count His virgin birth and resurrection.

We always have to keep in mind the key verse of this book.

JOHN 2:11- "This beginning of miracles did Jesus in Cana of Galilee, and manifested forth His glory; and His disciples believed on him."

There are two miracles that are actually listed as His first (*beginning*) and second miracles.

<u>Changing water into wine</u>:
JOHN 2:11 "This <u>beginning</u> of miracles did Jesus in Cana of Galilee, and manifested forth His glory; and His disciples believed on Him."

<u>Healing a Nobleman's child</u>:

<u>**JOHN 4:54**</u> "This is again the <u>second</u> miracle that Jesus did, when He was come out of Judaea into Galilee."

Without detailing the rest of the miracles Jesus preformed. I've compiled a small list.

Raising the dead on three occasions, Fed multitudes in the thousands twice, Walked on water, Healed various diseases, Cast out demons, Caught a fish with a coin in its mouth, Calmed storms, Curses a fig tree, Restores a severed ear and a withered hand. Catching of a large number of fish twice.

Jesus gave us the power to reform miracles too (*see 1Corinthians 12:10*).

<u>**MARK 9:38-40**</u> - "And John answered Him, saying, Master, we saw one casting out devils in thy name, and he followeth not us: and we forbad him, because he followeth not us. (V.39) But Jesus said, Forbid him not: for there is no man which shall do a miracle in my name, that can lightly speak evil of me. (V.40) For he that is not against us is on our part."

<u>**ACTS 19:11**</u>- "And God wrought special miracles by the hands of Paul."

<u>JESUS FORTELLS HIS DEATH</u>

<u>**LUKE 18:31-33**</u> - "Then He took unto Him the

twelve, and said unto them, Behold, we go up to Jerusalem, and all things that are written by the prophets concerning the Son of man shall be accomplished. (V.32) For He shall be delivered unto the Gentiles, and shall be mocked, and spitefully entreated, and spitted on: (V.33) And they shall scourge Him, and put Him to death: and the third day He shall rise again."

JESUS RIDES INTO JERUSALEM ON A DONKEY

ZECHARIAH 9:9 - "Rejoice greatly, O daughter of Zion; shout, O daughter of Jerusalem: behold, thy King cometh unto thee: He is just, and having salvation; lowly, and riding upon an ass, and upon a colt the foal of an ass."

MATTHEW 21:1-5 - "And when they drew nigh unto Jerusalem, and were come to Bethphage, unto the mount of Olives, then sent Jesus two disciples, (V.2) Saying unto them, Go into the village over against you, and straightway ye shall find an ass tied, and a colt with her: loose them, and bring them unto me. (V.3) And if any man say ought unto you, ye shall say, The Lord hath need of them; and straightway he will send them. (V.4) All this was done, that it might be fulfilled which was spoken by the prophet, saying, (V.5) Tell ye the daughter of Sion, Behold, thy King cometh unto thee, meek, and sitting upon an ass, and a colt the foal of an ass."

<u>JESUS CLEARING THE TEMPLE</u>

In this next account we find Jesus arriving in Jerusalem. Of course His first stop was the temple. Obviously He was upset by what He saw happening there. Did His emotions get the best of Him? No; once again He was fulfilling prophecy.

<u>**JOHN 2:13-17**</u> -And the Jews' Passover was at hand, and Jesus went up to Jerusalem, V.14 And found in the temple those that sold oxen and sheep and doves, and the changers of money sitting: V.15 And when He had made a scourge of small cords, He drove them all out of the temple, and the sheep, and the oxen; and poured out the changers' money, and overthrew the tables; V.16 And said unto them that sold doves, Take these things hence; make not my Father's house an house of merchandise. V.17 And his disciples remembered that it was written, The zeal of thine house hath eaten me up."

<u>**PSALM 69:9**</u> - "For the zeal of thine house hath eaten me up; and the reproaches of them that reproached thee are fallen upon me."

<u>A NEW COVENANT</u>

God made a Covenant with Noah never to destroy the Earth with a flood again.

GENESIS 9:13 - "I do set my bow in the cloud, and it shall be for a token of a covenant between me and the earth."

God also made a covenant with Abraham.

GENESIS 17:7 - "And I will establish my covenant between me and thee and thy seed after thee in their generations for an everlasting covenant, to be a God unto thee, and to thy seed after thee."

In Jeremiah, God says He's going to make a new covenant. This passage is known to be a summary of the covenant of grace made with believers in Jesus Christ. The writer of Hebrews refers to this passage in chapter eight, verses eight and nine.

JEREMIAH 31:31-33 - "Behold, the days come, saith the LORD, that I will make a new covenant with the house of Israel, and with the house of Judah: (V.32) Not according to the covenant that I made with their fathers in the day that I took them by the hand to bring them out of the land of Egypt;

which my covenant they brake, although I was an husband unto them, saith the LORD: (V.33) But this shall be the covenant that I will make with the house of Israel; After those days, saith the LORD, I will put my law in their inward parts, and write it in their hearts; and will be their God, and they shall be my people.

Jesus secured that new covenant for us by His death, burial, and resurrection.

MATTHEW 26:26-28 - "And as they were eating, Jesus took bread, and blessed it, and brake it, and gave it to the disciples, and said, Take, eat; this is my body. (V.27) And he took the cup, and gave thanks, and gave it to them, saying, Drink ye all of it; (V.28) For this is my blood of the new testament, which is shed for many for the remission of sins."

JESUS WASHES FEET

Have you ever heard someone say the best sermons are lived not preached? Jesus preached to His disciples many things. One of these was to be humble. Then He wanted them to see what being humble really was.

MARK 9:35 - "And he sat down, and called the twelve, and saith unto them, If any man desire to be first, the same shall be last of all, and servant of all."

MATTHEW 23:12 - "And whosoever shall exalt himself shall be abased; and he that shall humble himself shall be exalted."

JOHN 13:4&5 - "He riseth from supper, and laid aside His garments; and took a towel, and girded Himself. (V.5) After that He poureth water into a basin, and began to wash the disciples' feet, and to wipe them with the towel wherewith He was girded."

JOHN 13:12-17 - "So after He Had washed their feet, and had taken His garments, and was set down again, He said unto them, Know ye what I have done to you? (V.13) Ye call me Master and Lord: and ye say well; for so I am. (V. 14) If I then, your Lord and Master, have washed your feet; ye also ought to wash one another's feet. (V.15) For I have given you an example, that ye should do as I have done to you. (V.16) Verily, verily, I say unto you, The servant is not greater than his lord; neither he that is sent greater than he that sent him. (V.17) If ye know these things, happy are ye if ye do them."

Jesus' attitude of servanthood was in direct contrast to that of the disciples, who had recently been arguing among themselves as to which of them was the greatest (*Luke 22:24*). Since there was no servant present to wash their feet, it would never have occurred to them to wash one another's feet. When the Lord Himself stooped to this lowly task, they were stunned into silence. To his credit, though, Peter was profoundly uncomfortable with the Lord washing his feet, and, never being at a loss for words, Peter protested, "You shall never wash my feet!" (*But that is another story*).

Verse fifteen is the key verse I want to look at: "For I have given you an example, that ye should do as I have done to you." What was the example He wanted to give them? To your surprise, it was not to wash each others feet. But didn't He tell them "ye also ought to wash one another's feet"? Yes, however that was not the message that He wanted to teach them. It is the statement He made before He told them to wash each others feet. "Ye call me Master and Lord: and ye say well; for so I am. If I then, your Lord and Master, have washed your feet..." He was teaching them to be humble and serve others.

Many denominations have mistakenly taken these verses as a commandment from Jesus and participate in "foot washing services." Some of these foot washing services have been known to have helped to bring humility and forgiveness between dissenting brethren. There are many stories that have been told of church revivals which began from a good old fashioned foot washing service. Let me be the first to say, if you want to participate in foot washing services, go ahead (I have). However, there are questions that surround modern day foot washings as being Biblical. First the story only appears in John (which is not too surprising).There is a reference to it in First Timothy about a widow washing the saints feet (as was the custom of that day).

<u>**1 TIMOTHY 5:10**</u> - "Well reported of for good works; if she have brought up children, if she have lodged strangers, if she have washed the saints' feet, if she have relieved the afflicted, if she have diligently followed every good work."

This widow's practice of "washing the feet of the saints" speaks not of her involvement in a church ordinance but of her humble, slave-like service to other believers.

John states nowhere this should be a ritual of worship done in the assemblies of the church. Where does the Scripture say feet should be washed in a worship meeting or as an act of worship? Nothing is the passage says so. Any such conclusion is an assumption. No other passage gives any example or any indication that Christians did this in church worship assemblies. If Jesus intended this to be a religious ritual done in their assemblies, wouldn't we find examples of it being done, like we find examples of the Lord's Supper being done in assemblies? We have no instruction to do it as a church function, no instruction to do it in the worship assembly, we are never told what purpose any such act might serve, nor are we told when or how often to do it. When modern denominations attempt to practice "foot washing," that which they do is surely not what the Scriptures describe. In denominations people know ahead of time their feet will be washed, so they make sure they are clean! Who wants everybody in a church seeing and smelling your dirty feet? But this defeats the whole purpose of the washing, which was to meet a need as an act of humility. Jesus clearly said that what was already clean did not "need" to be washed. The feet washed in ritual ceremonies today are clean; therefore, by Jesus' own statement they need not be washed. His act was intended to meet a "need." Modern denominational ritual foot washing involves just the opposite: Feet are washed that do not need to be washed. So, the modern denominational ritual violates both aspects of what the Lord intended: It is not really an act of humility, and it does not really meet a need. It is nothing like what t Jesus really did.

<u>BEFORE GOINGTO THE CROSS</u>

<u>BETRAYED BY JUDAS ISCARIOT</u>

Did Jesus make a mistake in choosing Judas Iscariot as an apostle? No, it was all part of the master plan. It had to happen so the prophecy would be fulfilled.

<u>PSALM 41:9</u> - "Yea, mine own familiar friend, in whom I trusted, which did eat of my bread, hath lifted up his heel against me."

Unfortunately, this "familiar friend" was Judas

Iscariot.

LUKE 6:16 - "And Judas the brother of James, and Judas Iscariot, which also was the traitor."

MARK 14:18 - "And as they sat and did eat, Jesus said, Verily I say unto you, One of you which eateth with me shall betray me."

JOHN 13:18 - "I speak not of you all: I know whom I have chosen: but that the Scripture may be fulfilled, He that eateth bread with me hath lifted up his heel against me."

Although Jesus never named Judas Iscariot as the one who would betray Him. When asked "who is it?" He gave them a sign. It was obviously to all that Judas Iscariot was the one who received the bread from Jesus. Verse twenty-nine helps us understand why they didn't gang pile him, to stop him from betraying Jesus.

JOHN 13:25-27, 29 - "He (*John*) then lying on Jesus' breast saith unto Him, Lord, who is it? (V.26) Jesus answered, He it is, to whom I shall give a sop, when I have dipped it. And when He had dipped the sop, He gave it to Judas Iscariot, the son of Simon. (V.27) And after the sop Satan entered into him. Then said Jesus unto him, That thou doest, do quickly. (V.29) For some of them thought, because Judas had the bag, that Jesus had said unto him, Buy those things that we have need of against the feast; or, that he should give something to the poor."

Jesus taught the remaining eleven disciples from the end of Johns Chapter Thirteen to the end of Chapter Sixteen. Chapter Seventeen contains what is actually "The Lords' Prayer." This is where we have the proof that Jesus didn't make a mistake by choosing Judas Iscariot as one of His chosen twelve apostles. Remember John 13:18 said "I know whom I have chosen." Here in this passage of the prayer, Jesus wasn't making excuses to His Father. He was just telling Him it had to happen so "the scripture might be fulfilled."

JOHN 17:12 - "While I was with them in the world, I kept them in thy name: those that thou gavest me I have kept, and none of them is lost, <u>but the son of perdition</u>; that the scripture might be fulfilled."   (*Judas Iscariot*)

Peter confirmed this to the other disciples soon after Jesus ascended to heaven.

ACTS 1:16 - "Men and brethren, this scripture must needs have been fulfilled, which the Holy Ghost by the mouth of David spake before concerning Judas, which was guide to them that took Jesus."

PSALM 41:9 - "Yea, mine own familiar friend, in whom I trusted, which did eat of my bread, hath lifted up his heel against me."

JESUS PREDICTS PRTER'S DENIAL

Just as Jesus knew Judas Iscariot would betray Him. He knew Peter would deny Him; not once, not twice, but three times. Even though Jesus knew Peter would deny knowing Him. He also knew Peter would return to Him. Notice: Jesus didn't pray for Peter NOT to deny Him. He prayed that his faith failed not.

MATTHEW 26:34 - "Jesus said unto him, Verily I say unto thee, That this night, before the cock crow, thou shalt deny me thrice."

LUKE 22:31&32 - "And the Lord said, Simon, Simon, behold, Satan hath desired to have you, that he may sift you as wheat: (V.32) But I have prayed for thee, that thy faith fail not: and when thou art converted, strengthen thy brethren."

FORSAKEN BY DISCIPLES

MARK 14:27&49, 50 - "And Jesus saith unto them, All ye shall be offended because of me this night: for it is written, I will smite the shepherd, and the sheep shall be scattered. (V.49) I was daily with you in the temple teaching, and ye took me not: but the scriptures must be fulfilled. (V.50) And they all forsook Him, and fled."

<u>ZECHARIAH 13:7</u> - 'Awake, O sword, against my shepherd, and against the man that is my fellow, saith the LORD of hosts: smite the shepherd, and the sheep shall be scattered: and I will turn mine hand upon the little ones."

Contained in this passage is a story that is not in any of the other gospels. Here is an account of a certain unnamed young man. It would seem that he was not a disciple of Christ. However, some in the mob thought he was. As they grabbed him his cloth came off, and that's why he was naked.

<u>MARK 14:51& 52</u> - "And there followed Him a certain young man, having a linen cloth cast about his naked body; and the young men laid hold on him: (V.52) And he left the linen cloth, and fled from them naked."

There are speculations about who this young man was. Some say it was the author of this gospel, Mark himself (*since he was not an apostle*). Others say it may have been the rich young man that Jesus encountered in Matthew 19:20. Some even think it was the young man the women saw in the tomb of Jesus (*Mark 16:5*). This was an angel, so it couldn't have been him.

I personally believe that he lived near the

garden, perhaps in the house to which the garden belonged. Upon hearing the commotion in the garden he was frightened out of his bed, wrapping himself in a sheet he got up, and went to see what was going on. He saw a "multitude" of people, armed, and coming with such fury, and in the dead of night. In his quiet village, this would produce a great stir. This commotion alarmed the young man, who perhaps thought there was some sort of rioting in the city, or some uproar among the people. While standing there watching, some of the young men that came with the others, tried grabbing him too. Being that he was just wearing a sheet. He was able to run away leaving it in the hands of those who were attempting to take him.

Matthew and Luke, didn't see much point in mentioning it. It didn't seem to serve any purpose. It was just an unnecessary detail. So they intentionally left it out. I feel although it is an necessary detail that it should be mentioned, since it rarely is.

THE DEATH OF JUDAS ISCARIOT

There is much controversy surrounding the death of Judas Iscariot. First is the manner in which he took his life.

MATTHEW 27:5 - "And he cast down the pieces of silver in the temple, and departed, and went and hanged himself."

<u>**ACTS 1:18**</u> - "Now this man purchased a field with the reward of iniquity; and falling headlong, he <u>burst asunder in the midst, and all his bowels gushed out</u>."

This should not be taken as a contradiction if it is possible for both to be true.

Matthew records the mode in which Judas attempted his death by hanging. Peter speaks of the result. Since it scriptures don't say how long Judas was hanging. It is quite possible for Judas to have hung until his abdomen was partially decomposed; then his neck giving way, the rope breaking, or something else happened which caused his body to fall. It burst open when it struck the ground. People will say "When the rope breaks, you don't fall headfirst." That's actually not entirely true. It's proven; if the rope snaps, it jerks back on the body and the feet go up and the head goes down.

The second issue is the money. In Acts, Peter was talking and said "this man purchased a field." In Matthew, it says "he cast down the pieces of silver in the temple." How could he (Judas) buy a field if he gave the money back?

<u>**MATTHEW 27:3**</u> - "Then Judas, which had betrayed Him, when he saw that He was condemned, repented himself, and brought again the thirty pieces of silver to the chief priests and elders."

Judas is said to have purchased the field, and so he did. For the priests bought the land with his money, so that legally made it his purchase.

ACTS 1:18 - "Now this man purchased a field with the reward of iniquity."

MATTHEW 27:7-10 - "And they took counsel, and bought with them the potter's field, to bury strangers in. (V.8) Wherefore that field was called, The field of blood, unto this day. (V.9) Then was fulfilled that which was spoken by Jeremy the prophet, saying, And they took the thirty pieces of silver, the price of Him that was valued, whom they of the children of Israel did value; (V.10) And gave them for the potter's field, as the Lord appointed me."

WHERE DID THEY TAKE JESUS

I was made aware there was a discrepancy on where the mob took Jesus from the garden. Matthew, Mark and Luke all state that Jesus was taken to Caiaphas the high priest. Luke adds that it was "into the high priest's house" (*Luke 22:54*).

MATTHEW 26:57 - "And they that had laid hold on Jesus led Him away to Caiaphas the high priest."

The discrepancy is what you find in John. It

says they went to Annass' first.

JOHN 18:13 - "And led Him away to Annas first; for he was father in law to Caiaphas, which was the high priest that same year."

I don't know why people feel there is a contradiction here. Once again three of the four say they took Jesus to Caiaphas. If you read on to verse nineteen, you will find Caiaphas questioning Jesus; so obviously, they took Jesus to Caiaphas. The fact they led Him away to Annas first, is a mute point. Suppose you're taking a trip to the mall. You have to get in your car first. Most people won't point that out (Matthew, Mark and Luke). John thought it was important enough to write down!

So you could say He was brought to Caiaphas by way of Annas. If you want to get technical; Luke states that Annas and Caiaphas were both the high priests (*Luke3:2*).

FALSE WITNESSES

PSALM 35:11 - "False witnesses did rise up; they laid to my charge things that I knew not."

MARK 14:57&58 - "And there arose certain, and bare false witness against Him, saying, (V.58) We heard Him say, I will destroy this temple that is made with hands, and within three days I will build another made without hands."

<u>PETER DENIES KNOWING JESUS</u>

We've already discussed earlier how that Peter would deny knowing Jesus. Here we will discuss seemed contradictions surrounding this subject. Did the cock crow once, twice, or as sometimes stated three times? When was it that the cock crowed? We will look at the four accounts from the epistles. First reviewing what Jesus told Peter.

<u>**MATTHEW 26:34**</u> - "Jesus said unto him, Verily I say unto thee, That this night, before the cock crow, thou shalt deny me thrice."

<u>**MATTHEW 26:74&75**</u> - "Then began he to curse and to swear, saying, I know not the man. And immediately the cock crew). (V.75) And Peter remembered the word of Jesus, which said unto him, "<u>Before the cock crow</u>, thou shalt deny me thrice." And he went out, and wept bitterly."

<u>**MARK 14:30**</u> - "And Jesus saith unto him, Verily I say unto thee, That this day, even in this night, <u>before the cock crow twice</u>, thou shalt deny me thrice."

<u>**MARK 14:66-72**</u> -And as Peter was beneath in the palace, there cometh one of the maids of the high priest: (V.67) And when she saw Peter warming himself, she looked upon him, and said,

And thou also wast with Jesus of Nazareth V.68) But he denied, saying, I know not, neither understand I what thou sayest. And he went out into the porch; and <u>the cock crew</u>. (V.69) And a maid saw him again, and began to say to them that stood by, This is one of them. (V.70) And he denied it again. And a little after, they that stood by said again to Peter, Surely thou art one of them: for thou art a Galilaean, and thy speech agreeth thereto. (V.71) But he began to curse and to swear, saying, I know not this man of whom ye speak. (V.72) And <u>the second time the cock crew</u>. And Peter called to mind the word that Jesus said unto him, <u>Before the cock crow twice</u>, thou shalt deny me thrice. And when he thought thereon, he wept."

<u>LUKE 22:34</u> - "And He said, I tell thee, Peter, <u>the cock shall not crow this day</u>, before that thou shalt thrice deny that thou knowest me."

<u>LUKE 22:60&61</u> - "And Peter said, Man, I know not what thou sayest. And immediately, while he yet spake, <u>the cock crew</u>. (V.61) And the Lord turned, and looked upon Peter. And Peter remembered the word of the Lord, how He had said unto him, <u>Before the cock crow</u>, thou shalt deny me thrice."

<u>JOHN 13:38</u> - "Jesus answered him, Wilt thou lay down thy life for my sake? Verily, verily, I say unto thee, <u>The cock shall not crow</u>, till thou hast denied me thrice."

JOHN 18:25-27 - "And Simon Peter stood and warmed himself. They said therefore unto him, Art not thou also one of His disciples? He denied it, and said, I am not. (V.26) One of the servants of the high priest, being his kinsman whose ear Peter cut off, saith, Did not I see thee in the garden with Him? (V.27) Peter then denied again: and immediately <u>the cock crew</u>."

The fact that Peter would deny knowing Jesus three times is consistent; and the fact that Peter did deny Him three times is also consistent. The questions posed are; did the cock crow once or twice, and when was it that the cock crowed? Mark is the only one who states that Jesus said "before the cock crow twice." The other three say that Peter would have already denied Him three times before the cock crows. I really don't see a contradiction here. Once again, we are dealing with four individual viewpoints. Here is the bombshell though. Mark was not an apostle. He got most of his information from Peter. Jesus told Peter, and Peter told Mark. The other apostles left Jesus at the garden. John was the only other one who was there*. However, he was with Jesus and maybe didn't notice the first crowing of the cock.

JOHN 18:15- "And Simon Peter followed Jesus, and so did another disciple*: that disciple (*John*) was known unto the high priest, and went in with Jesus into the palace of the high priest."

*John several times in this gospel speaking of himself as another disciple. Also "the disciple Jesus loved."

BARABBAS

There is one person in the life of Jesus that gets way more credit than he deserves, this is Barabbas; which is strange because He is mentioned in all four Gospels. The popular belief is that Jesus took the place of Barabbas and was crucified instead of him. This couldn't be further than the truth. It was foreordained that Jesus was to be crucified. He knew He was going to die, and knew how it was going to happen. This is made evident by the words He spoke to His disciples,

MATTHEW 20:19 - "And shall deliver Him to the Gentiles to mock, and to scourge, and to crucify Him: and the third day He shall rise again."

JOHN 12:32&33- "And I, if I be lifted up from the earth, will draw all men unto me. (V.33) This He said, signifying what death He should die." (*Crucifixion*)

In fact, He knew it was at this time that these things would come to pass.

MATTHEW 26:45 - "Then cometh He to His disciples, and saith unto them, Sleep on now, and take your rest: <u>behold, the hour is at hand</u>, and the Son of man is betrayed into the hands of sinners."

Speaking of time, let's look at the account now, then discuss it when we have the facts.

MATTHEW 27:15-26 - "Now at that feast the governor (*Pilate*) was wont to release unto the people a prisoner, whom they would. (V.16) And they had then a notable prisoner, called Barabbas. (V.17)Therefore when they were gathered together, Pilate said unto them, Whom will ye that I release unto you? Barabbas, or Jesus which is called Christ? (V.20) But the chief priests and elders persuaded the multitude that they should ask Barabbas, and destroy Jesus. (V.21) The governor answered and said unto them, Whether of the twain (two) will ye that I release unto you? They said, Barabbas. (V.22)Pilate saith unto them, What shall I do then with Jesus which is called Christ? They all say unto him, Let Him be crucified. (V.26) Then released he Barabbas unto them: and when he had scourged Jesus, he delivered Him to be crucified."

So, He wasn't taking the place of anyone. It wasn't like Jesus went to Barabbas and said "I'll take your place." Likewise, Pilate didn't choose Barabbas as the one to be released. It could have been any of the other prisoners being held that was released. Barabbas just happened to be the one the people were persuaded to ask for (*John 18:40-"Then cried they all again, saying, Not this man, but Barabbas."*).

It was kind of strange they would ask for him. Mark said that he was bound (*in jail*) for insurrection (*which means rebellion*), and while in this insurrection he had committed murder. Luke says basically the same thing about him, and John calls him a robber. It's in Matthew that he is called "Notable." This means the people knew who he was and what he did. Yet they asked for Him to be released and Jesus to be crucified. Not in his place, just to be crucified!

<u>ACTS 3:14</u> - "But ye denied the Holy One and the Just, and desired a murderer to be granted unto you."

Barabbas is not mentioned before this incident, nor is he mentioned by name after it. The gospels don't say what he did after he was released. That is why I say He gets way more credit than he deserves.

<u>ON HIS WAY TO THE CROSS</u>

<u>ISAIAH 53:7&8</u> - "He was oppressed, and He was afflicted, yet He opened not His mouth: He is brought as a lamb to the slaughter, and as a sheep before her shearers is dumb, so He openeth not His mouth. V.8 He was taken from prison and from judgment: and who shall declare his generation? for he was cut off out of the land of the living: for the transgression of my people was he stricken."

ACTS 8:32 - "The place of the scripture which He read was this, He was led as a sheep to the slaughter; and like a lamb dumb before his shearer, so opened He not His mouth."

With the betrayal, trials, scourging, and rejection behind Him, Jesus is finally headed to His destiny, to complete what He came here to do. It was no surprise to Jesus what was about to happen. He laid out the details to His disciples before they happened.

MATTHEW 20:18& 19 - "Behold, we go up to Jerusalem; and the Son of man shall be betrayed unto the chief priests and unto the scribes, and they shall condemn him to death, (V.19) And shall deliver him to the Gentiles to mock, and to scourge, and to crucify him: and the third day he shall rise again."

Jesus is now carrying His cross, and on His way to be crucified. We find three different accounts of this one event. John tells us. Jesus carried His cross, alone all the way to Golgotha (*Calvary*).

JOHN 19:16&17 - "Then delivered he Him therefore unto them to be crucified. And they took Jesus, and led him away. (V.17) And He bearing His cross went forth into a place called the place of a skull, which is called in the Hebrew Golgotha."

Luke relates basically the same story. However, he adds that two malefactors (*thieves or evildoers*) were with Him; on their way to be crucified also.

LUKE 23:32&33 - "And there were also two other, malefactors, led with Him to be put to death. (V.33) And when they were come to the place, which is called Calvary, there they crucified Him."

Mark and Matthew added a detail the other two failed to mention. Many think Jesus carried His cross by Himself all the way to Calvary. In fact I've heard ministers say "Jesus carried His cross all the way to Calvary, and didn't give up. Now don't you give up." The real fact of the matter is that Jesus was beaten, and abused so badly. He couldn't carry the cross by Himself. The Roman soldiers saw this; and enlisted a man called Simon to either help Jesus carry His cross, or to carry it for Him. I believe it was more of a "let's get this done" act, than one of compassion.

MARK 15:20& 21 - "And when they had mocked Him, they took off the purple from Him, and put His own clothes on Him, and led Him out to crucify Him. (V.21) And they compel one Simon a Cyrenian, who passed by, coming out of the country, the father of Alexander and Rufus, to bear His cross."

MATTHEW 27:32 - "And as they came out, they found a man of Cyrene, Simon by name: him they compelled to bear His cross."

Again we find no contradictions. When you combine the facts from all four of the Gospels. The account of Jesus' trip to the cross is quite easy to explain. I see it like this. Jesus and the two others were carrying their crosses, start out for the place where they will be crucified. Seeing the weight of the cross was too much for Jesus to bear alone. The soldiers compelled Simon (*of Cyrene*) to bear His cross, and they continue on to Calvary.

THE LAST WORDS OF JESUS

The last thing Jesus did before He died was what is called "The seven sayings from the cross."We know that Jesus gave up the ghost (*died*) on the cross, and did of course not speak until He was resurrected. However, He had a little more to say while He hung on the cross.

LUKE 23:34 - "Then said Jesus, Father, forgive them; for they know not what they do. And they parted his raiment, and cast lots."

<u>LUKE 23:42&43</u> - "And he said unto Jesus, Lord, remember me when thou comest into thy kingdom. (V.43) And Jesus said unto him, Verily I say unto thee, To day shalt thou be with me in paradise."

<u>MARK 15:34</u> - "And at the ninth hour Jesus cried with a loud voice, saying, Eloi, Eloi, lama sabachthani? which is, being interpreted, My God, my God, why hast thou forsaken me?"

<u>JOHN 19:25-27</u>- "Now there stood by the cross of Jesus His mother, and His mother's sister, Mary the wife of Cleophas, and Mary Magdalene. (V.26) When Jesus therefore saw His mother, and the disciple standing by, whom he loved, He saith unto His mother, Woman, behold thy son! (V.27) Then saith He to the disciple, Behold thy mother! And from that hour that disciple took her unto his own home."

<u>JOHN 19:28</u> - "After this, Jesus knowing that all things were now accomplished, that the scripture might be fulfilled, saith, I thirst."

<u>LUKE 23:46</u> - "And when Jesus had cried with a loud voice, He said, Father, into thy hands I commend my spirit: and having said thus, he gave up the ghost."

<u>**JOHN 19:30**</u> - "When Jesus therefore had received the vinegar, He said, It is finished: and He bowed His head, <u>and gave up the ghost</u>."

Here is what He said in a nutshell. First He asked His Father (*God*) to forgive those who took part in His crucifixion because they didn't know the magnitude of what they were doing. (*1Corinthians 2:8b "for had they known it, they would not have crucified the Lord of glory"*). Then after all it was prophesied that He would die this way; (*John 12:32 &33: "And I, if I be lifted up from the earth, will draw all men unto me. (V.33) This He said, signifying what death He should die"*). The fact that He asked forgiveness for those persecuting Him led one of the thieves to repent. This led to the second statement, He assured us that to be absent from the body is to be present with the Lord (*2 Corinthians 5:8*). The third saying was a hard one for Him. The reason He was hanging on the cross was to pay for our sins. Not only paying for our sins, but the Bible tells us in 2 Corinthians 5:21; "For He hath made Him to be sin for us, who knew no sin."

God had to turn His back on sin. Jesus couldn't understand why His Father turned His back on Him.

Fourthly, He took care of His mothers needs. The disciple whom he loved was John. It is said that she lived with him twelve years and then died.

The fifth saying was Him fulfilling the last prophecy concerning His life before He died. He said "I thirst."

PSALM 22:15 -My strength is dried up like a potsherd; and my tongue cleaveth to my jaws; and thou hast brought me into the dust of death.

PSALM 69:21 -They gave me also gall for my meat; and in my thirst they gave me vinegar to drink.

The six and seventh sayings must have came one after the other. He commended His spirit to His Fathers hands; and "He said, It is finished: and he bowed Hs head, and gave up the ghost."

The guards came to break His legs, but found that He was already dead.

WHEN HE DIED

When Jesus "gave up the ghost." Many might think that's the end of the story. He will be buried, (*and for us who believe, will be resurrected in three days*). However, there were a few things which happened that bear our looking into them.

Firstly, and this happened while He was still alive, until His death. The sun refused to shine form1twelve noon until three PM.

MATTHEW 27:45 - "Now from the <u>sixth hour</u> there was darkness over all the land unto the <u>ninth</u>

<u>hour</u>."

The fact that this actually happened is confirmed by historians. This is a good thing, however I choose to trust what the Bible has to say about this. What happened is actually another prophesy being fulfilled.

<u>AMOS 8:9</u> - "And it shall come to pass in that day, saith the Lord GOD, that <u>I will cause the sun to go down at noon</u>, and I will darken the earth in the clear day."

In case you didn't catch it. The sixth hour is noon. This can't be a coincidence.

As I said earlier. The darkness was occurring before He died, up to the point of His death. It's what happened when He died that brought fear to those who were watching that day.

<u>MATTHEW 27:50-54</u> - "Jesus, when He had cried again with a loud voice, yielded up the ghost. (V.51) And, <u>behold, the veil of the temple was rent in twain</u> from the top to the bottom; and <u>the earth did quake, and the rocks rent</u>; (V.52) And the <u>graves were opened;</u> and many bodies of the saints which slept arose, (V.53) And <u>came out of the graves</u> after his resurrection, and went into the holy city, and <u>appeared unto many</u>. (V.54) Now when the centurion, and they that were with him, watching Jesus, saw the earthquake, and those things that were done, they feared greatly, saying, Truly this was the Son of God."

Let's look at each of these happenings separately.

The first thing listed is the veil in the temple being torn in two (*rent in twain*). You probably overlooked the second word in verse fifty one; It is "behold." This word reveals what a amazing thing had just happened. The word means "Turn aside, and see this great sight, and be astonished at it." Be astonished by how this was done, from the top to the bottom. I believe God did this; and it was done in this manner to prevent anyone from saying men did it. The veil was opened to show that all now have access to the throne of God, not just the priests. Speaking of the priests. They would have been there going about their duties when this occurred. So, they would have been the ones to have seen it happen.

Next listed was the earthquake. This was also included in the prophecy of Amos.

<u>AMOS 8:8</u> - "<u>Shall not the land tremble</u> for this, and <u>every one mourn that dwelleth therein?</u> and it shall rise up wholly as a flood; and it shall be cast out and drowned, as by the flood of Egypt."

That must have been something to have been there on that day! Unexplained darkness, and an earthquake, and graves opening. No wonder the people feared greatly. Apparently, because of the ground shaking, it unearthed some graves. There is much speculation about what actually happened here. Even though the graves were opened, and the bodies arose. It wasn't until Jesus was resurrected (*3 days later*) that they "went into the holy city, and appeared unto many." Some think that they arose only to bear witness of Christ's resurrection to those to whom they appeared, and, having finished their testimony, retired to their graves again. We may have many questions concerning it, which we cannot resolve: as; Who these saints were, that arose. Some think, the ancient prophets, that were buried in the land of Canaan. Others think, these that arose were modern saints, that had been with Jesus in the flesh, but died before him; as His father Joseph, Zecharias, Simeon, John Baptist, and others. Perhaps they were saints, who in the Old-Testament times had believed and as Hebrews 11:13 puts it: "died in faith, not having received the promises." So, to whom did they appeared (*not to all the people it is certain, but to many*), in what manner did they appear, how often, what they said and did, and how they disappeared, are secret things which we have no answer for; we must not fabricate what is not written.

Let's take another look at verse fifty four to wrap this section up.

<u>MATTHEW 27:54</u> - "Now when the centurion,

and <u>they that were with him</u>, watching Jesus, saw the earthquake, and those things that were done, <u>they</u> feared greatly, saying, Truly this was the Son of God."

We've already stated how the priests were the ones to see the veil split. Everyone else was out watching the crucifixion. They were the ones who saw these events taking place. From what I see. The centurion was not the only one to say "Truly this was the Son of God." Then the soldiers came to brake His legs, and the others with Him.

JOHN 19:32-37 - "Then came the soldiers, and brake the legs of the first, and of the other which was crucified with Him. (V. 33) But when they came to Jesus, and saw that He was dead already, they brake not His legs: (V34) But one of the soldiers with a spear pierced His side, and forthwith came there out blood and water. (V.35) And he that saw it bare record, and his record is true: and he knoweth that he saith true, that ye might believe. (V.36) For these things were done, that the scripture should be fulfilled, A bone of him shall not be broken. (V.37) And again another scripture saith, They shall look on Him whom they pierced."

There was one last thing left to do; bury the body of Jesus. This was done by two men who were followers of Jesus, but secretly, Joseph of

Arimathaea and Nicodemus.

JOHN 19:38-40 - "And after this Joseph of Arimathaea, being a disciple of Jesus, but secretly for fear of the Jews, besought Pilate that he might take away the body of Jesus: and Pilate gave him leave. He came therefore, and took the body of Jesus. (V.39) And there came also Nicodemus, which at the first came to Jesus by night, and brought a mixture of myrrh and aloes, about an hundred pound weight. (V.40) Then took they the body of Jesus, and wound it in linen clothes with the spices, as the manner of the Jews is to bury."

These were the last people to see Jesus before He was laid in the tomb. All four Gospel writers mention Joseph of Arimathaea, but only in this context. He is not mentioned before or after this account. We do know that he was instrumental in fulfilling the prophecy of Isaiah 53:9: "And He made His grave with the wicked, and with the rich in His death." This is shown to us in Matthew.

MATTHEW 27:57&60 - "When the even was come, there came a rich man of Arimathaea, named Joseph, who also himself was Jesus' disciple (V. 60) And laid it in his own new tomb, which he had hewn out in the rock: and he rolled a great stone to the door of the sepulchre, and departed."

Nicodemus however is another story. His name is only found in John, but in three different places. He is referred to as the one "who came to Jesus at night." John 7:50 says that one of them (*meaning a follower*). Most people don't even know that He was at the tomb with Joseph of Arimathaea. As I said he is only mentioned in John.

I don't know about being a secret follower of Jesus, but both men are blessed with having an important part in the life of Jesus.

So, the body of Jesus was buried; and three days later He was resurrected from the dead. (See more on this in the Chapters "DEATH, BURIAL RESURRECTION")

POST RESURRECTION

Jesus didn't go straight to heaven when He was resurrected. He spent another forty days here on earth. (*Acts 1:3: "To whom also He showed Himself alive after His passion by many infallible proofs, being seen of them <u>forty days</u>, and speaking of the things pertaining to the kingdom of God"*). One reason Jesus remained on earth forty days after His resurrection instead of ascending immediately into heaven was to demonstrate (*prove*) to His followers that He was truly alive. On most of the occasions Jesus showed Himself He gave His disciples the opportunities of testing the fact of His resurrection. He conversed with them face to face. They touched Him, and He ate bread with them. Below we will look at the appearances of Jesus after He was resurrected. We will start with 1 Corinthians 15:4-7. It is a sort of an catch- all of those saw the risen savior; but not without controversy.

<u>1 CORINTHIANS 15:4-7</u> - "And that He was buried, and that He rose again the third day according to the scriptures: (V.5) And that He was seen of Cephas (Peter), then of the twelve: (V.6) After that, He was seen of above five hundred brethren at once; of whom the greater part remain unto this present, but some are fallen asleep. (V.7) After that, He was seen of James; then of all the apostles."

The first thing I noticed was the no mention of the women. As we see later the Bible clearly tells us in Mark 16:9: "He appeared first to Mary Magdalene." Then Matthew 28:9 tells us someone called "the other Mary" was with her, and saw (*and held*) Him too! However, Paul failed to mention this. We are told Cephas (*who was Peter*), was the first one to see Him. I don't doubt that Peter saw Jesus after He was resurrected, but he certainly was not the first person to see Him. Besides this, we have no other references recorded in any of the Gospels of this encounter. Now, I did say "I don't doubt that Peter saw Jesus after He was resurrected." I don't mean with the other disciples present. Some say he (*Peter*) was one of the men Jesus met on the road to Emmaus. This can't be true; when they went back to tell the disciple that they had seen Jesus, we are told they "found the eleven gathered together." Judas was dead, so these had to be the eleven apostles. There are still some who go on to say it could have been eleven others, and not Peter. However, the verse goes on to say "and them that were with them (*Luke 24:33*)." Then comes to statement in question: Luke 24:34 "Saying, The Lord is risen indeed, and hath appeared to Simon." Now, if one of them was Peter, they wouldn't have worded it that way. So, why do I believe that Peter had a private meeting with the risen Jesus? When the women were at the sepulchre, "they saw a young man (*an angel*) sitting on the right side, clothed in a long white garment."

<u>MARK 16:6& 7</u> - And he saith unto them, Be not affrighted: Ye seek Jesus of Nazareth, which was crucified: He is risen; He is not here: behold the place where they laid (V.7) But go your way, tell His disciples <u>and Peter </u>that He goeth before you into Galilee: there shall ye see Him, as He said unto you.

Once again I need to mention. While every Scripture is inspired of God, Peter related much of what happened to Mark. None of the other four Gospels makes mention of Peter being named separately from the other disciples. Matthew wrote that the angel told the women to "go quickly, and tell His disciples;" no mention of Peter specifically.

There is the possibility that Jesus in his wonderful grace, had taken an opportunity early that day (*though where, or in what manner, is not recorded*) to show Himself to Peter, that He might early relieve his distresses and fears, on account of having so shamefully denied his Master. Nonetheless He appeared to Simon (*Peter*).

As mentioned above, The Bible credits Mary Magdalene as the first one to see Jesus after He was resurrected from the dead.

MARK 16:9 - "Now when Jesus was risen early the first day of the week, He appeared first to Mary Magdalene, out of whom He had cast seven devils."

JOHN 20:14-17 - "And when she had thus said, she turned herself back, and saw Jesus standing, and knew not that it was Jesus. (V.15) Jesus saith unto her, Woman, why weepest thou? whom seekest thou? She, supposing Him to be the gardener, saith unto Him, Sir, if thou have borne Him hence, tell me where thou hast laid Him, and I will take Him away. (V.16) Jesus saith unto her, Mary. She turned herself, and saith unto Him, Rabboni; which is to say, Master. (V.17) Jesus saith unto her, Touch me not."

I said Mary Magdalene gets the credit as the first one to see Jesus after He was resurrected. That is true, but no entirely. As the late Paul Harvey used to say, "And now, the rest of the story." Mary Magdalene, Mary the mother of James, and Salome all went to the sepulchre to anoint the body of Jesus. After the angel had spoken to them; Mark 16:8 tell us "And they went out quickly, and fled from the sepulchre." I can't say the other women outran Mary Magdalene, and she alone saw Jesus, as recorded by John. Matthew 28:9 tells us all the women saw Him.

<u>MATTHEW 28:9</u> - "And as they went to tell His disciples, behold, Jesus met them, saying, All hail. And <u>they</u> came and held Him by the feet, and worshipped Him."

This is not a contradiction. I believe John just left out the other women. In Johns account, he ends it abruptly with Jesus telling Mary Magdalene "Touch me not." Compare this with where Matthew says "And they came and held Him by the feet." This sounds like the same story to me! If I may quote another newscaster it would have to be Walter Cronkite. He always ended by saying "And that's the way it is."

Back in 1 Corinthians 15:5 we're told He was next seen by the twelve. They were called this, even though Judas was no longer among them, it was because this was their usual number. There is a section of scripture that is often overlooked, which might prompt you to ask; where did he show himself to them first? Matthew passes over several other appearances of Christ, recorded by Mark, Luke and John. In each of these, the disciples are eating in Jerusalem when Jesus appears to them. Matthew finds them going to a mountain in Galilee. Apparently Jesus had told them to meet Him there (Mark 16:7).

MATTHEW 28:10 - "Then said Jesus unto them (the women), Be not afraid: go tell my brethren that they go into Galilee, and there shall they see me."

MATTHEW 28:16 - "Then the eleven disciples went away into Galilee, into a mountain where Jesus had appointed them."

The place was a mountain in Galilee, was probably the same mountain on which He was transfigured. There they met, for privacy. The Gospel of Matthew ends at Chapter twenty nine, so it doesn't mention the dinners. This must have been the first encounter with Jesus after He arose.

As I mentioned in Mark, Luke and John, we find the disciples eating in Jerusalem when Jesus appears to them. Here are those accounts.

MARK 16:14- "Afterward He appeared unto the eleven as they sat at meat, and upbraided them with their unbelief and hardness of heart, because they believed not them which had seen Him after He was risen."

LUKE 24:33-36 - "And they rose up the same hour, and returned to Jerusalem, and found the eleven gathered together, and them that were with them, (V.34) Saying, The Lord is risen indeed, and hath appeared to Simon. (V.35) And they told what things were done in the way, and how He was known of them in breaking of bread. (V.36) And as they thus spake, Jesus Himself stood in the midst of them, and saith unto them, Peace be unto you."

JOHN 20:19&20, 24 - "Then the same day at evening, being the first day of the week, when the doors were shut where the disciples were assembled for fear of the Jews, came Jesus and stood in the midst, and saith unto them, Peace be unto you. (V.20) And when He had so said, He showed unto them his hands and his side. Then were the disciples glad, when they saw the Lord. (V.24) But Thomas, one of the twelve, called Didymus, was not with them when Jesus came."

The Gospel of Mark ends after dinner with Jesus charging them to "Go ye into all the world, and preach the gospel to every creature," and ascending up to heaven. So obviously, he left some parts out. Luke and John confirm this was the same encounter, with Jesus showing them the marks from His wounds.

LUKE24:39 - "Behold my hands and my feet, that it is I myself: handle me, and see; for a spirit hath not flesh and bones, as ye see me have."

JOHN 20:20- "And when He had so said, He showed unto them his hands and His side. Then were the disciples glad, when they saw the Lord.

Did you notice that in the account of the dinner by John I included verse twenty four? This is because I wanted you to know that Thomas was not there when Jesus came. This is how he received the nickname "Doubting Thomas." I'm not sure if Jesus came to remove Thomas's doubt, or something else, but He spent the bulk of His time talking with Him. The point is He appeared to them again.

JOHN 20:26 - "And after eight days again His disciples were within, and Thomas with them: then came Jesus, the doors being shut, and stood in the midst, and said, Peace be unto you."

Paul also failed to mention a couple of men who encountered Jesus on the road to Emmaus. These are the ones who come to Jerusalem and told the disciples "The Lord is risen indeed, and hath appeared to Simon."Then "told what things were done in the way, and how He was known of them in breaking of bread." The whole story is found in Luke 24:13- 32.

MARK 16:12 -"After that He appeared in another form unto two of them, as they walked, and went into the country."

Jesus showed Himself to the disciples when they were fishing on sea of Tiberias.

John referrers to this appearance as "the third time that Jesus showed Himself to His disciples." The whole story is found in John 21:1-14. I chose to use just four verses to highlight this event.

JOHN 21:1, 5, 9, 14 - "After these things Jesus showed Himself again to the disciples at the sea of Tiberias; and on this wise showed He Himself." (V.5) "Then Jesus saith unto them, Children, have ye any meat? They answered him, No." (V.9) "As soon then as they were come to land, they saw a fire of coals there, and fish laid thereon, and bread." (V.14) "This is now the third time that Jesus showed Himself to His disciples, after that He was risen from the dead."

Paul made mention in1 Corinthians 15:6 that, "He was seen of above five hundred brethren at once." We are not told when, where or to who this was. The occasions listed in this book are the only ones I can find in the Bible, which is the ultimate source for this study. This doesn't mean it didn't happen though. We have to keep in mind the key verse behind this book is John 21:25: "And there are also many other things which Jesus did, the which, if they should be written every one, I suppose that even the world itself could not contain the books that should be written."

The last we see of Jesus here on earth is on Mt. Olivet (*Acts1:12*) where He ascended to heaven.

MARK16:19 - "So then after the Lord had spoken unto them, He was received up into heaven, and sat on the right hand of God."

ACTS 1:9 - "And when He had spoken these things, while they beheld, He was taken up; and a cloud received him out of their sight."

Let's go back to Paul's list of people who saw Jesus after He was resurrected. In verse eight he list himself: 1Corinthians 15:8 "And last of all He was seen of me also, as of one born out of due time." Now according to scripture there is one last person who saw the resurrected Jesus; Paul the Apostle. Paul himself was last of all favored with the sight of Him. Not a vision, while Saul was on one of his deadly errands to Damascus, the living Jesus personally appeared to him. This undeniable encounter with the resurrected Lord revolutionized Saul's life. Because of this Paul continued with verse nine; "For I am the least of the apostles, that am not meet to be called an apostle, because I persecuted the church of God." Yes Paul became an Apostle. He told Timothy it was "by the commandment of God our Saviour, and Lord Jesus Christ (*1Timothy 1:1*). God made him an apostle. It was one of the peculiar offices of an apostle to be a witness of our Saviour's resurrection (*Acts 1:22*) So; Paul was called into the apostolical office, being made evident by the Lord Jesus appearing to him on his way to Damascus (*Acts 9:1-9*).

This is the life of Jesus (on earth)!

Luke 24:44 - *"And he said unto them, These are the words which I spake unto you, while I was yet with you, that all things must be fulfilled, which were written in the law of Moses, and in the prophets, and in the psalms, concerning me."*

THE CHILDHOOD OF JESUS

The Bible doesn't give us much information about Jesus before his ministry began. While the book of Matthew gives many details about the birth of Jesus. Luke gives us a more insightful view into His childhood. Below are two passages found only in Luke with reference to Jesus as a child.

LUKE 2:21&22 - "And when eight days were accomplished for the circumcising of the child, His name was called JESUS, which was so named of the angel before he was conceived in the womb. (V.22) And when the days of her purification according to the law of Moses were accomplished, they brought Him to Jerusalem, to present Him to the Lord."

LUKE 2:40-52 - "And the child grew, and waxed strong in spirit, filled with wisdom: and the grace of God was upon Him. (V.41) Now His parents went to Jerusalem every year at the feast of the Passover. (V.42) And when He was twelve years old, they went up to Jerusalem after the custom of the feast. (V.43) And when they had fulfilled the days, as they returned, the child Jesus tarried behind in Jerusalem; and Joseph and His mother knew not of it. (V.44) But they, supposing Him to have been in the company, went a day's journey; and they sought Him among their kinsfolk and acquaintance. (V.45) And when they found Him not, they turned back again to Jerusalem, seeking Him. (V.46) And it came to pass, that after three days they found Him in the temple, sitting in the midst of the doctors, both hearing them, and asking them questions. (V.47) And all that heard

Him were astonished at his understanding and answers. (V.48) And when they saw Him, they were amazed: and his mother said unto Him, Son, why hast thou thus dealt with us? behold, thy father and I have sought thee sorrowing. (V.49) And He said unto them, How is it that ye sought me? wist ye not that I must be about my Father's business? (V.50) And they understood not the saying which He spake unto them. (V.51) And He went down with them, and came to Nazareth, and was subject unto them: but His mother kept all these sayings in her heart. (V.52) And Jesus increased in wisdom and stature, and in favour with God and man."

SIMEON & ANNA

When Joseph and Mary brought Jesus to Jerusalem so they could present Him to the Lord. Luke introduces us to two people who are worthy of being mentioned. These two seemingly irrelevant people played an important role in declaring who Jesus was. They are not to be found anywhere else in the Bible, nor are they mentioned after their encounter with Jesus. God blessed both of them. They were rewarded for waiting to see the Christ (*The Redemption of Jerusalem*).

LUKE 2:25-30 - "And, behold, there was a man in Jerusalem, whose name was Simeon; and the same man was just and devout, waiting for the consolation of Israel: and the Holy Ghost was upon him. (V.26) And it was revealed unto him by the Holy Ghost, that he should not see death, before he had seen the Lord's Christ. (V.27) And he came by the Spirit into the temple: and when the parents brought in the child Jesus, to do for him after the custom of the law, (V.28) Then took he him up in his arms, and blessed God, and said, (V.29) Lord, now lettest thou thy servant depart in peace, according to thy word: (V.30) For mine eyes have seen thy salvation.

LUKE 2:36-38 - "And there was one Anna, a prophetess, the daughter of Phanuel, of the tribe of Aser: she was of a great age, and had lived with an husband seven years from her virginity; (V.37) And she was a widow of about fourscore and four years, which departed not from the temple, but served God with fastings and prayers night and day. (V.38) And she coming in that instant gave thanks likewise unto the Lord, and spake of Him to all them that looked for redemption in Jerusalem."

Simeon was told by the Holy Ghost that he should not die, before he had seen the Lord's Christ (*The Messiah*). When he saw Jesus, and held Him. Simeon knew this child was the one he was waiting for, and now he could die in peace. Anna, who was always at the temple, observing the dedication of Jesus; being a prophetess understood who and what this child was, went on to proclaim this good news.

Joseph and Mary had been through many radical changes in the past months, not to mention the past days. They must have had many questions on their minds. Luke tells us that when the shepherds left the stable, "Mary kept all these things, and pondered them in her heart (*Luke 2:19*)." Simeon and Anna helped provide some reassurance this was all in God's will.

<u>SINLESS</u>

I've heard preachers try to talk about Jesus as a child and say something along these lines; "Jesus was an ordinary child, He'd do the things that boys do." and so on. Well I have a problem with that. I know what boys do! We are told Jesus never sinned, that means never!

<u>2 CORINTHIANS 5:21</u> - "For He hath made Him to be sin for us, who knew no sin."

<u>1JOHN 3:5</u> - "And ye know that He was manifested to take away our sins; and in Him is no sin."

I'm not saying He stayed home in the kitchen with Mary. In fact He spent most of His time with Joseph. He is referred to as "the carpenter" in Mark 6:3. Think of the story from Luke where it said "Jesus tarried behind in Jerusalem." We see that His parents left to go home "supposing Him to have been in the company." You can only come to the conclusion that Jesus wasn't a problem child. They didn't even notice that He wasn't with them!

THE ONLY BEGOTTEN?

There are many people who believe Jesus was the only child Mary gave birth to.

Once again; they're not reading the rest of the story. Jesus is referred to as "The only begotten Son" (of God), not the only begotten of Mary. Speaking of Mary; it's interesting to note that nowhere in the Bible does it refer to her as "The Virgin Mary" (whereas Rahab was always called "the harlot").This is because after having Jesus, Mary was no longer a virgin! In the following scripture we see that after Jesus was born, Joseph "knew" (had intercourse) with Mary for the first time.

MATTHEW 1:25 - "And knew her not till she had brought forth her firstborn son: and he called His name JESUS."

After the birth of Jesus. Mary became pregnant with Joseph's children. Jesus had brothers and sisters.

MARK 6:3 - "Is not this the carpenter, the son of Mary, the brother of James, and Joses, and of Juda, and Simon? and are not his sisters here with us?”

<u>**WHAT ABOUT JOSEPH?**</u>

The Bible contains a little more information about the life of Joseph; that it does about the childhood of Jesus, but not much. In Matthew (2:19), the last mention of Joseph was when an angel appeared to Him in Egypt. Mark doesn't mention him at all. John makes mention of him twice. Luke writes the most about him. Along with recording the birth of Jesus; he tells us Joseph was in Jerusalem when Jesus was twelve years old. From then on there are no concrete details of whether he was alive or had died. Below are some times he was referenced to, it is speculation if he was alive or just being referenced to.

<u>LUKE 3:23</u> - “And Jesus himself began to be about thirty years of age, being (<u>as was supposed</u>) <u>the son of Joseph</u>, which was the son of Heli.”

Just because it says “the son of,” it doesn't mean Joseph was alive. If you read on you'll see that phrase used 74 more times in verses 24-38.

I need to note that Luke is actually detailing the linage of Jesus through Mary. However, in biblical days, women were not accredited for much. So, when it says “Joseph, which was the son of Heli.” It really means Heli was Joseph's father-in-law. This is shown in Matthews writing of

Jesus' linage through Joseph (*Matthew 1:16: "And Jacob begat Joseph the husband of Mary, of whom was born Jesus, who is called Christ"*).

LUKE 4:22 -"And all bare Him witness, and wondered at the gracious words which proceeded out of His mouth. And they said, Is not this <u>Joseph's son?</u>"

JOHN 1:45 - "Philip findeth Nathanael, and saith unto him, We have found Him, of whom Moses in the law, and the prophets, did write, Jesus of Nazareth, <u>the son of Joseph</u>."

JOHN 6:42 - "And they said, Is not this Jesus, <u>the son of Joseph</u>, whose father and mother we know? how is it then that he saith, I came down from heaven?

(John mentions Joseph twice and only as "Jesus, the son of Joseph")

DEATH, BURIAL & RESURRECTION

1CORINTHIANS 15:3-4- *"For I delivered unto you first of all that which I also received, how that Christ died for our sins according to the scriptures; (V.4) And that He was buried, and that He rose again the third day according to the scriptures."*

BEFORE THE CROSS

Jesus suffered what is called "horrific" treatment at the hands of the Romans while He was in their custody. The prophet Isaiah foretold the "what" and the "why" of this ordeal.

ISAIAH 53:4-5 - "Surely He hath borne our griefs, and carried our sorrows: yet we did esteem Him stricken, smitten of God, and afflicted. (V.5) But He was wounded for our transgressions, He was bruised for our iniquities: the chastisement of our peace was upon Him; and with His stripes we are healed."

Jesus fulfilled three prophecies that came from one verse. The following tells the tell us what they were, and result of the abuse He suffered.

ISAIAH 50:6 - "I gave my back to the smiters,

and my cheeks to them that plucked off the hair: I hid not my face from shame and spitting."

He was beaten beyond recognition:

ISAIAH 52:14- "As many were astonied (*appalled*) at thee; his visage was so marred more than any man, and his form more than the sons of men."

New Living Translation:
ISAIAH 52:14 - "But many were amazed when they saw Him. His face was so disfigured He seemed hardly human, and from His appearance, one would scarcely know He was a man."

The gospels recall not only the physical abuse Jesus was put through, but the emotional abuse also. Matthew wrote verses that used phrases such as these, "And they that passed by reviled Him, wagging their heads", "Likewise also the chief priests mocking Him, with the scribes and elders" and "He trusted in God; let Him deliver Him now" (*Matthew 27:39, 41&43*). Do you think Jesus was surprised that they would treat Him (*The Son Of God*) like that? No, and according to this verse, He was expecting it!

PSALM 22:6-8 - "But I am a worm, and no man; a reproach of men, and despised of the people. (V.7) All they that see me laugh me to scorn: they shoot out the lip, they shake the head, saying, (V.8) He trusted on the LORD that He would deliver Him: let Him deliver Him, seeing he delighted in Him."

THE SIGN ON THE CROSS

Here is a prime example of how nitpicky people can get. They claim there are inconsistencies about what was written on the sign that hung on the cross. Those who are looking for contradictions just want to say, "See, the Bible is full of mistakes!" and choose to reject it entirely as being untrustworthy. So, as is our practice, we'll go to the Word.

MATTHEW 27:37 - "And set up over His head His accusation written, THIS IS JESUS THE KING OF THE JEWS."

MARK 15:26 - "And the superscription of His accusation was written over, THE KING OF THE JEWS."

LUKE 23:38 - "And a superscription also was written over Him in letters of Greek, and Latin, and Hebrew, THIS IS THE KING OF THE JEWS."

JOHN 19:19&20b - "And Pilate wrote a title, and put it on the cross. And the writing was,

JESUS OF NAZARETH THE KING OF THE JEWS. (V.20b) and it was written in Hebrew, and Greek, and Latin."

Let's first look at the sign itself. Mark tells us that a superscription was written; Matthew, says that it was set up over His head; Luke, that it was written in three languages; and John tells that Pilate was the writer. All these statements are correct, even though each writer says something different! We must remember there was only one sign. There would be no contradiction if the sign simply said, "This is Jesus of Nazareth the King of the Jews." Luke and John, tell us that the inscription on the Cross of Jesus was written in three languages, Greek, Latin and Hebrew. Isn't it a reasonable assumption that the Gospel writers chose to quote what was written in one of the different languages? Here is where the harmony of the gospels comes back into play. Putting all four together, you would once again get "This is Jesus of Nazareth the King of the Jews."

<u>ON THE CROSS</u>

After Jesus had been beaten beyond recognition, spit on, beard pulled out, mocked, and utterly disrespected. You would think they were through with Him.

But no, the worst was yet t come. It was not only the pain of crucifixion, but the humiliation of it too. Paul wrote in Galatians "for it is written, Cursed is every one that hangeth on a tree" (*Galatians 3:13, Deuteronomy 21:23*). You may not realize it but Jesus was not wearing the little loin cloth that is depicted in movies, and paintings. He was stripped naked, for all to see, including His Mother. That was part of the shame of crucifixion. The cloth was added to pictures and movies so not to offend the people viewing it. Everything that happened on the cross had already been prophesied to come to pass. Jesus was fully aware of this. That is made evident by the words He prayed while in the garden "O my Father, if it be possible, let this cup pass from me: nevertheless not as I will, but as thou wilt."

We will now go through the chain of events that led to our saviours' death (*the occurrence and the prophesy relating to it*).

Numbered with the transgressors:
LUKE 23:32 - "And there were also two other, malefactors, led with Him to be put to death."

MARK 15:28 - "And the scripture was fulfilled, which saith, And He was numbered with the transgressors."

ISAIAH 53:12 - "Therefore will I divide Him a portion with the great, and He shall divide the spoil with the strong; because He hath poured out His soul unto death: and He was numbered with the transgressors; and He bare the sin of many, and made intercession for the transgressors."

The procedure of crucifying:
JOHN 19:37 - "And again another scripture saith, They shall look on Him whom they pierced."

JOHN 20:25 - "The other disciples therefore said unto him, We have seen the Lord. But he (*Thomas*) said unto them, Except I shall see in His hands the print of the nails, and put my finger into the print of the nails, and thrust my hand into His side, I will not believe."

PSALM 22:16 - "For dogs have compassed me: the assembly of the wicked have enclosed me: they pierced my hands and my feet."

ZECHARIAH 13:6 - "And one shall say unto Him, What are these wounds in thine hands? Then He shall answer, Those with which I was wounded in the house of my friends."

Casting lots for His Clothing:
JOHN 19:24 - "They said therefore among themselves, Let us not rend it, but cast lots for it, whose it shall be: that the scripture might be fulfilled, which saith, They parted my raiment among them, and for my vesture they did cast lots. These things therefore the soldiers did."

PSALM 22:18 - "They part my garments among them, and cast lots upon my vesture."

Jesus Thirsts:
JOHN 19:28 - "After this, Jesus knowing that all things were now accomplished, that the scripture might be fulfilled, saith, I thirst."

JOHN 19:29 - "Now there was set a vessel full of <u>vinegar</u>: and they filled a sponge with vinegar, and put it upon hyssop, and put it to His mouth."

PSALM 22:15 - "My strength is dried up like a potsherd; and <u>my tongue cleaveth to my jaws</u>; and thou hast brought me into the dust of death."

PSALM 69:21 - "They gave me also <u>gall</u> for my meat; and in my thirst they <u>gave me vinegar to drink</u>."

<u>No Bone Broken</u>:

JOHN 19:32-33 - "Then came the soldiers, and brake the legs of the first, and of the other which was crucified with Him. (V.33) But when they came to Jesus, and saw that He was dead already, <u>they brake not His legs</u>."

JOHN 19:36 - "For these things were done, that the scripture should be fulfilled, <u>A bone of him shall not be broken</u>."

PSALM 34:20 - "He keepeth all his bones: <u>not one of them is broken</u>."

<u>THE LAST WORDS JESUS SPOKE WHILE ON THE CROSS</u>

I was made aware of yet another supposed contradiction. What were last words Jesus spoke while on the cross? As our practice is, let's look at what was written.

MATTTHEW 27:46, 50 - "And about the ninth

hour Jesus cried with a loud voice, saying, Eli, Eli, lama sabachthani? that is to say, My God, my God, why hast thou forsaken me? (V.50) Jesus, when He had cried again with a loud voice, yielded up the ghost."

LUKE 23:46 - "And when Jesus had cried with a loud voice, He said, Father, into thy hands I commend my spirit: and having said thus, He gave up the ghost."

JOHN 19:30 - "He (*Jesus*) said, It is finished: and He bowed his head, and gave up the ghost."

Each of these sections of scripture ended with "gave (or yielded) up the ghost." That statement means He died. However, the context of each section is different, except for crying with a loud voice. Is there a contradiction then? No; I believe He said all three! Let's put it together like this. About the ninth hour Jesus cried with a loud voice, saying, "My God, my God, why hast thou forsaken me? Then said, Father, into thy hands I commend my spirit. It is finished": and He bowed His head, and gave up the ghost. It can be found to be very simple if you look at it as three separate statements, as opposed to one or two that don't say the same thing.

There is a service some churches hold on Good Friday. It is called "The Seven Sayings From The Cross." Where seven speakers (usually Pastors), give a short message on one of the saying they were assigned to speak on. These verses are considered to be the three last sayings.

DEATH

JOSEPH OF ARIMATHAEA

Joseph of Arimathaea played an interesting role in the life of Jesus. He unknowingly was responsible for fulfilling the last Messianic prophecy before the resurrection of Jesus. He is mentioned in all four gospels. All four tell the same story, here is the account found in Matthew.

MATTHEW 27:57-60 - "When the even was come, there came a rich man of Arimathaea, named Joseph, who also himself was Jesus' disciple: (V.58) He went to Pilate, and begged the body of Jesus. Then Pilate commanded the body to be delivered. (V.59) And when Joseph had taken the body, he wrapped it in a clean linen cloth, (V.60) And laid it in his own new tomb, which he had hewn out in the rock: and he rolled a great stone to the door of the sepulchre, and departed."

As mentioned above, Joseph of Arimathaea is mentioned in all four gospels. However, other than this one instance, he is not mentioned before or after it. With this in mind; it can safely be said that Jesus did not tell Joseph to bury Him in his new tomb, so the prophecy would be fulfilled. Matthew stated that Joseph was a disciple of Jesus. Although Joseph believed in Jesus, he did not openly profess it. His disciples had fled, and had no means to provide a proper burial. Joseph stepped up and placed him in his own new sepulchre. I'm sure Joseph did this out of the goodness of his own heart, giving no mind that in doing so; he would be fulfilling this prophecy.

<u>ISAIAH 53:9</u> - "And He made his grave with the wicked, and with the rich in His death; because He had done no violence, neither was any deceit in His mouth."

<u>JESUS IN HELL</u>

Here we have yet but another highly controversial subject. Did Jesus go to Hell while He was dead? Maybe the question should be; what did Jesus do while He was in the tomb? I believe He did indeed go to hell. We'll get to the scriptures in a minute. But, figure this; He took my sins upon Him. He died in my place on the cross. Why wouldn't He take my place in Hell too? He gave me eternal life, and I'm a sinner! Now for the controversy; preachers will tell you "the Bible doesn't tell you He went to Hell." It does say He "went to the lower parts of the earth." Let's look at that then. Jesus said in Matthew, He would be "in the heart (*center*) of the earth." The center of the Earth is 5,700 to 9,000 degrees. Even if He did go to the "lower parts" like Ephesians says. The Crust of the Earth can reach 1,600 degrees. The Mantle, which is below that is up to 4,000 degrees, and molten. The Outer Core is below that, which reaches over 5,000 degrees. So, how low did Jesus go into the earth?

MATTHEW 12:40 - "For as Jonas (*Jonah*) was three days and three nights in the whale's belly; so shall the Son of man be three days and three nights <u>in the heart (*center*) of the earth</u>."

EPHESIANS 4:8-10 - "Wherefore He saith, When He ascended up on high, He led captivity captive, and gave gifts unto men. (V.9) (Now that He ascended, what is it but that He also descended first into <u>the lower parts of the earth</u>? (V.10) He that descended is the same also that ascended up far above all heavens, that He might fill all things."

Those same preachers will tell you the lower parts of the earth meant inside the tomb. You see the tomb was "hewn out in the rock (*Matthew 27:60*)".This means it must have to been somewhat underground. Good point, but that doesn't sound all too low. My question is; how does what Peter wrote fit into that theory?

1 PETER 3:18-19 - "For Christ also hath once suffered for sins, the just for the unjust, that He might bring us to God, being put to death in the flesh, but quickened by the Spirit: (V.19) By which also He went and preached unto the spirits in prison."

How could He have "preached unto the spirits in prison," If He was lying in a tomb? Jesus hadn't been resurrected yet. This meant the "spirits" were the saints who died in faith, not having received the promise (*Hebrews 11:13*). The prison was Hell (*Abraham's bosom - Luke 16:22*). He had to go to them, since they couldn't come to Him. Notice where the text says, "being put to death in the flesh, but quickened by the Spirit." This is to say Jesus' body was dead, and He went in the Spirit. Now, one last point; about those preachers who tell you "the Bible doesn't tell you Jesus went to hell" (or does it?). On the day of Pentecost, Peter preached a powerful sermon. In it he referred to a passage David wrote in the book of Psalm. Below is the statement and the verse in reference.

<u>**ACTS 2:25-27 &31**</u> - "For David speaketh concerning Him, I foresaw the Lord always before my face, for He is on my right hand, that I should not be moved: (V.26) Therefore did my heart rejoice, and my tongue was glad; moreover also my flesh shall rest in hope: (V.27) Because <u>thou wilt not leave my soul in hell</u>, neither wilt thou suffer thine Holy One to see corruption.
(V.31) He seeing this before spake of the

resurrection of Christ, that His soul was not left in hell, neither His flesh did see corruption."

PSALMS 16:10 - "For <u>Thou wilt not leave my soul in hell</u>; neither wilt thou suffer thine Holy One to see corruption."

Look at the first line in Acts. It says "concerning Him (*Jesus*)." Why would Peter and David refer to Jesus not being left in hell if He didn't go there? Some have said David wrote this about himself. However, when comparing scripture with scripture, it's clear He was writing about the Messiah (*Jesus*).

RESURRECTION

JOHN 20:9 -*"For as yet they knew not the scripture, that He must rise again from the dead."*

THE STONE ROLLED AWAY

To set the stage for the next topic; I want to take a quick look at the stone that was placed at the tomb. Matthew and Mark both state that a stone was rolled to the door of the sepulchre. However, all four gospels do state that the stone was rolled away. There is some controversy of how the stone was moved from the door. Matthew clears that matter up in his writings.

MATTHEW 27:60 - "And laid it in his (*Joseph of Arimathaea*) own new tomb, which he had hewn out in the rock: and he rolled a great stone to the door of the sepulchre, and departed."

MATTHEW 28:2 - "And, behold, there was a great earthquake: for the angel of the Lord descended from heaven, and came and rolled back the stone from the door, and sat upon it."

THE WOMEN AT THE TOMB

The list of women, who came to the tomb, is another hot topic for skeptics. As we did for the apostles, let's go to the word and see who was listed.

MATTHEW 28:1 - "Mary Magdalene and the other Mary."

MARK 16:1- "Mary Magdalene, and Mary the mother of James, and Salome."

LUKE 24:1- "they, and certain others with them."

<u>**JOHN 20:1**</u>- "Mary Magdalene"

I can see why this topic may raise some questions. Matthew says two were there. Mark says three, Luke has no certain number, and John has just one. This isn't really a big problem if you use a little common sense. Remember, each writer was inspired by God what to write down (*2Timothy 3:16, 2 Peter 1:20&21*).God is not wrong, and He knows who was there. Here is where we got to use our common sense. Have you ever been to, or seen an event, live or televised, where certain celebrities were said to have been in attendance? They were mentioned as being there, but what about the hundreds or thousands that were there also, but were not mentioned at all. Only God knows for certain which women came to the tomb that morning.

There is even still more controversy surrounding these women other than who was there. Who did they see?

<u>**MATTHEW 28:2-5**</u> - "And, behold, there was a great earthquake: for the angel of the Lord descended from heaven, and came and rolled back the stone from the door, and sat upon it. (V.3) His countenance was like lightning, and his raiment white as snow: (V.4) And for fear of him the keepers did shake, and became as dead men. (V.5) And the angel answered and said unto the women, Fear not ye: for I know that ye seek Jesus, which

was crucified.

MARK 16:5 - "And entering into the sepulchre, they saw a young man sitting on the right side, clothed in a long white garment; and they were affrighted."

LUKE 24:4 - "And it came to pass, as they were much perplexed thereabout, behold, two men stood by them in shining garments."

JOHN 20:12 - "And seeth two angels in white sitting, the one at the head, and the other at the feet, where the body of Jesus had lain."

WHO RAISED JESUS?

Hopefully you are not like the Sadducees; and believe in the resurrection of the dead; the resurrection of Jesus in particular. It's not a myth or a fable. The Greeks had a word for resurrection; Anastasis (*an-as'-tas-is*). Why would there be a word for something that couldn't happen? Jesus was resurrected from the dead!

God knew it:
1 PETER 1:18-20 - "Forasmuch as ye know that ye were not redeemed with corruptible things, as silver and gold, from your vain conversation received by tradition from your fathers; (V.19) But

with the precious blood of Christ, as of a lamb without blemish and without spot: (V.20) Who verily was foreordained before the foundation of the world, but was manifest in these last times for you."

<u>Jesus knew it</u>:

<u>MATTHEW 16:21</u> - "From that time forth began Jesus to show unto his disciples, how that He must go unto Jerusalem, and suffer many things of the elders and chief priests and scribes, and be killed, and be raised again the third day."

<u>We know it</u>; by believing what is written in the Bible is the word of God. Luke wrote the book of Acts. He recorded the history of the early church, including what was said by "the fathers of our faith." I'd like us to look at Acts and what Peter and Paul (*Acts 13:37*) had to say about the resurrection of Jesus; here is undeniable evidence that God indeed raised Him from the dead.

<u>ACTS 2:23&24</u> -"Him, being delivered by the determinate counsel and foreknowledge of God, ye have taken, and by wicked hands have crucified and slain: (V.24) Whom God hath raised up, having loosed the pains of death: because it was not possible that He should be holden of it."

<u>ACTS 2:32</u> - "This Jesus hath God raised up, whereof we all are witnesses."

ACTS 3:15 - "And killed the Prince of life, whom God hath raised from the dead; whereof we are witnesses."

ACTS 3:26 - "Unto you first God, having raised up His Son Jesus, sent Him to bless you, in turning away every one of you from his iniquities."

ACTS 4:10 - "Be it known unto you all, and to all the people of Israel, that by the name of Jesus Christ of Nazareth, whom ye crucified, whom God raised from the dead, even by Him doth this man stand here before you whole."

ACTS 5:30 - "The God of our fathers raised up Jesus, whom ye slew and hanged on a tree."

ACTS 10:40 - "Him God raised up the third day, and showed Him openly."

ACTS 13:29&30 - "And when they had fulfilled all that was written of Him, they took Him down from the tree, and laid him in a sepulchre. (V.30) But God raised Him from the dead."

ACTS 13:33 - "God hath fulfilled the same unto us their children, in that He hath raised up Jesus again; as it is also written in the second psalm, Thou art my Son, this day have I begotten thee."

ACTS 13:37 - "But He, whom God raised

again, saw no corruption."

As I stated above here is the undeniable evidence that God indeed raised Jesus from the dead. Not to press the point, but when Paul wrote his letters to the churches he stated nineteen more times that God raised Jesus from the dead, mostly in his letters to the Romans, and to the Corinthians. These were all written after Jesus had been resurrected and ascended to heaven.

There is a point I want to look into though. When Jesus was alive and living here on earth, He made it sound like He was going to raise Himself. Notice how He used the pronoun of "I."

JOHN 2:19 - "Jesus answered and said unto them, Destroy this temple, and in three days I will raise it up."

JOHN 10:17 &18 - "Therefore doth my Father love me, because I lay down my life, that I might take it again. (V.18) No man taketh it from me, but I lay it down of myself. I have power to lay it down, and I have power to take it again. This commandment have I received of my Father."

JOHN 11:25 - "Jesus said unto her, I am the resurrection, and the life: he that believeth in me, though he were dead, yet shall he live."

So; did God raise Jesus, or did He do it

Himself? The answer is "yes." You only have to look at two verses to understand the reason why the answer is yes.

MATTHEW 1:23- "Behold, a virgin shall be with child, and shall bring forth a son, and they shall call his name Emmanuel, which being interpreted is, God with us.

JOHN 14:8&9 - "Philip saith unto him, Lord, show us the Father, and it sufficeth us. (V.9) Jesus saith unto him, Have I been so long time with you, and yet hast thou not known me, Philip? he that hath seen me hath seen the Father; and how sayest thou then, Show us the Father?"

If you're still confused; the explanation is that while Jesus was here on earth, He was God in flesh. The Bible tells us in Matthew 28:2 that an angel of the Lord rolled back the stone from the door, but it was God the Father who raised Him up from the dead (Acts 3:26 - "Unto you first God, having raised up His Son Jesus).

MATTHEW 28:2 - "And, behold, there was a great earthquake: for the angel of the Lord descended from heaven, and came and rolled back the stone from the door, and sat upon it."

ROMANS 10:9 - "That if thou shalt confess with thy mouth the Lord Jesus, and shalt believe in thine heart that God hath raised him from the dead, thou shalt be saved."

LUKE 24:44 - "And He said unto them, These are the words which I spake unto you, while I was yet with you, that all things must be fulfilled, which were written in the law of Moses, and in the prophets, and in the Psalms, concerning me."

JOHN 2:22 - "When therefore He was risen from the dead, His disciples remembered that He had said this unto them; and they believed the scripture, and the word which Jesus had said."

EVERLASTING KINGDOM

PSALM 145:13 - "Thy kingdom is an everlasting kingdom, and thy dominion endureth throughout all generations."

JOHN 18:36 - "Jesus answered, My kingdom is not of this world: if my kingdom were of this world, then would my servants fight, that I should not be delivered to the Jews: but now is my kingdom not from hence."

LUKE 1:32&33 - "He shall be great, and shall be called the Son of the Highest: and the Lord God shall give unto Him the throne of His father David: (V.33) And He shall reign over the house of Jacob for ever; and of His kingdom there shall be no end."

If Jesus had not been resurrected (*raised from the dead*), how could He have an everlasting kingdom?

LUKE 24:45 - *"Then opened He their understanding, that they might understand the scriptures."*

ROMANS 15:4 - *"For whatsoever things were written aforetime were written for our learning, that we through patience and comfort of the scriptures might have hope."*

THE RESURRECTION

JOHN 11:25&26- "Jesus said unto her (*Martha*), I am the resurrection, and the life: he that believeth in me, though he were dead, yet shall he live: (V.26) And whosoever liveth and believeth in me shall never die. Believest thou this?"

I do realize I just ended with a study on the resurrection. However I feel that I that I need to look a little bit deeper into the subject.

The birth and death of Jesus wouldn't have meant much if He hadn't been resurrected from the dead. We all are born and we all will die. If Jesus hadn't been resurrected, He would have been a man like everyone else. He would have been known as a prophet, and we could visit His tomb. The difference is His tomb is empty.

Jesus accomplished many major feats while here on earth. He was born of a virgin, healed multitudes, raised the dead, and died for our sins. All off these are amazing and I thank Him for them. However, there is one thing that He did which I consider to be the most important. He was resurrected from the dead! The resurrection of Jesus is the signal most significant thing He did. All the other things He did hinge on His being raised from the dead.

In his first letter to the Corinthians, Paul dedicated nearly the whole fifteenth chapter pertaining to the statement I just made. In verse nineteen he wrote "If in this life only we have hope in Christ, we are of all men most miserable." The reason for this is because of what he wrote in the verses which preceded that statement.

<u>1 CORINTHIANS 15:13-18</u> - "But if there be no resurrection of the dead, then is Christ not risen: (V.14) And if Christ be not risen, then is our preaching vain, and your faith is also vain. (V.15) Yea, and we are found false witnesses of God;

because we have testified of God that He raised up Christ: whom He raised not up, if so be that the dead rise not. (V.16) For if the dead rise not, then is not Christ raised: (V.17) And if Christ be not raised, your faith is vain; ye are yet in your sins. (V.18) Then they also which are fallen asleep in Christ are perished."

Did you notice all the repercussions if Jesus had not been raised from the dead? As mentioned above how He died for our sins. According to verse seventeen; if Christ was not raised, our faith is in vain and we are still in our sins. All those who have (*and will*) died, are decaying in the grave. Meaning if Jesus wasn't raised neither will we be. If Jesus wasn't resurrected there would be no need for church or bibles, and all who preach the resurrection of the dead would be false prophets.

<u>1 CORINTHIANS 15:3&4</u> - "For I delivered unto you first of all that which I also received, how that Christ died for our sins according to the scriptures; (V.4) And that He was buried, and that He rose again the third day according to the scriptures."

I do realize how some may see the resurrection of the dead to be impossible. The Sadducees were of this group (*that is why they were sad you see*). Matthew 22:23 tells us "The same day came to him the Sadducees, which say that there is no resurrection." We know that with God nothing is impossible! When the Christian "dies," the Bible calls it "sleep." We already have life and shall not "die."

JOHN 5:24 - "Verily, verily, I say unto you, He that heareth My word, and believeth on Him that sent Me, hath everlasting life, and shall not come into condemnation; but is passed from death unto life."

Because of our belief in Jesus we are "passed from death unto life." Below are two examples of what this means.

JOHN 8:51-53 - "Verily, verily, I say unto you, If a man keep my saying, he shall never see death. (V.52) Then said the Jews unto Him, Now we know that thou hast a devil. Abraham is dead, and the prophets; and thou sayest, If a man keep my saying, he shall never taste of death. (V.53) Art thou greater than our father Abraham, which is dead? and the prophets are dead: whom makest thou thyself?"

LUKE 21:16-19 - "And ye shall be betrayed both by parents, and brethren, and kinsfolks, and friends; and some of you shall they cause to be put to death. (V.17) And ye shall be hated of all men for my name's sake. (V.18) But there shall not an hair of your head perish. (V.19) In your patience possess ye your souls."

How could some lose their heads, and yet not lose a hair? It is a proverbial expression, expressing the greatest security imaginable; it is frequently used both in the Old Testament and New. Some think that it refers to the preservation of the lives of all the Christians. To this end Jesus said in Mathew 10:30: "the very hairs of your head are all numbered." An account of them is kept, so that none of them shall perish where He will miss it. When you come to balance profit and loss, you will find that nothing has perished at all, but, on the contrary, that you have great gain in the joys of a life eternal.

I'd imagine the best example of our resurrection because of our belief in Jesus is shown in what is called the "rapture." We truly are blessed to be provided with such in depth details of this great occurrence.

<u>1 CORINTHIANS 15:51-53</u> - "Behold, I show you a mystery; We shall not all sleep, but we shall all be changed, (V.52) In a moment, in the twinkling of an eye, at the last trump: for the trumpet shall sound, and the dead shall be raised incorruptible, and we shall be changed. (V.53) For this corruptible must put on incorruption, and this mortal must put on immortality."

1 THESSALONIANS 4:13-17- "But I would not have you to be ignorant, brethren, concerning them which are asleep, that ye sorrow not, even as others which have no hope. (V.14) For if we believe that Jesus died and rose again, even so them also which sleep in Jesus will God bring with him. (V.15) For this we say unto you by the word of the Lord, that we which are alive and remain unto the coming of the Lord shall not prevent them which are asleep. (V.16) For the Lord Himself shall descend from heaven with a shout, with the voice of the archangel, and with the trump of God: and the dead in Christ shall rise first: (V.17) Then we which are alive and remain shall be caught up together with them in the clouds, to meet the Lord in the air: and so shall we ever be with the Lord."

All this is possible because Jesus indeed did rise from death. I say death not sleep, because He paid the price for our sins. Romans 6:23says "For the wages of sin is death." He died so we won't have to. There is a second half Romans 6:23, it says: "but the gift of God is eternal life through Jesus Christ our Lord."

1 THESSALONIANS 1:10 - "And to wait for His Son from heaven, whom He raised from the dead, even Jesus, which delivered us from the wrath to come."

1 CORINTHIANS 15:20 - "But now is Christ

risen from the dead, and become the firstfruits of them that slept."

<u>THE BLOOD OF JESUS</u>

You can't have a book about Jesus and fail to mention His Blood. The main purpose Jesus came to Earth as a man was so that He could die (*bleed*), and be the sacrifice for our sins. It may sound strange, but He lived, so He could die (*for us*). Below is a list of benefits provided to us by His blood.

<u>**MATTHEW 26:28**</u> - "For this is my blood of the new testament, which is shed for many for the remission of sins."

<u>**ROMANS 3:25**</u> -"Whom God hath set forth to be a propitiation through faith in His blood, to declare His righteousness for the remission of sins that are past, through the forbearance of God."

<u>**ROMANS 5:9-10**</u> - "Much more then, being now justified by His blood, we shall be saved from wrath through Him. (V.10) For if, when we were enemies, we were reconciled to God by the death

of His Son, much more, being reconciled, we shall be saved by His life."

EPHESIANS 1:7 - "In whom we have redemption through His blood, the forgiveness of sins, according to the riches of His grace."

COLOSSIANS 1:14 - "In whom we have redemption through His blood, even the forgiveness of sins."

HEBREWS 9:22 - "And almost all things are by the law purged with blood; and without shedding of blood is no remission."

1 JOHN 1:7 "But if we walk in the light, as He is in the light, we have fellowship one with another, and the blood of Jesus Christ His Son cleanseth us from all sin."

REVELATION 1:5b - "Unto Him that loved us, and washed us from our sins in His own blood."

In the Old Testament under the Mosaic Law God demanded a sacrifice for the sins of the people. In the New Testament God sent Jesus to be the sacrifice for our sins. This was actually a fulfillment of a little known Messianic promise. Abraham was asked by God to offer his son Isaac for a burnt offering. While they were on their way

Isaac said "Behold the fire and the wood: but where is the lamb for a burnt offering? (*Genesis 22:7*)."

GENESIS 22:8 "And Abraham said, My son, God will provide Himself a lamb for a burnt offering: so they went both of them together."

GENESIS 22:13 - "And Abraham lifted up his eyes, and looked, and behold behind him a ram caught in a thicket by his horns: and Abraham went and took the ram, and offered him up for a burnt offering in the stead of his son.

The promise was that "God will provide Himself a lamb;" and we know that Jesus is "the Lamb of God."

There is something in verse thirteen that is vitally important. Notice that the ram (*lamb*) was "caught in a thicket by his horns." The reason this is so important is because a sacrifice had to have no broken bones. If it had been caught by a leg, it might have broke one while trying to get free. Just as our lamb Jesus was to have no broken bones (*Psalm 34:20*). Also it was to be free of spot or blemish. (*1 Peter 1:19: "But with the precious blood of Christ, as of a lamb without blemish and without spot"*). So you see that by being caught by his horns was to way to keep the lamb acceptable for a sacrifice. Speaking of which; God sent the perfect sacrifice.

HEBREWS 10:4-6 - "For it is not possible that the blood of bulls and of goats should take away sins. (V.5) Wherefore when he cometh into the world, He saith, Sacrifice and offering thou wouldest not, but a body hast thou prepared Me: (V.6) In burnt offerings and sacrifices for sin thou hast had no pleasure."

Jesus became our High Priest. The former priests came to atone for the sins of the people every year, and they were constantly moving about performing ceremonial rites. Unlike the high priests up to this time, Jesus completed His work the first time.

HEBREWS 10:10-12 - "By the which will we are sanctified through the offering of the body of Jesus Christ once for all. (V.11) And every priest standeth daily ministering and offering oftentimes the same sacrifices, which can never take away sins: (V.12) But this man, after He had offered one sacrifice for sins for ever, sat down on the right hand of God."

HEBREWS 9:9-14 - "Which was a figure for the time then present, in which were offered both gifts and sacrifices, that could not make him that did the service perfect, as pertaining to the conscience; (V.10) Which stood only in meats and drinks, and divers washings, and carnal ordinances, imposed on them until the time of reformation. (V.11) But Christ being come an high priest of good things to come, by a greater and more perfect tabernacle, not made with hands, that is to say, not of this building; (V.12) Neither by the blood of goats and calves, but by His own blood He entered in once into the holy place, having obtained eternal redemption for us. (V.13) For if the blood of bulls and of goats, and the ashes of an heifer sprinkling the unclean, sanctifieth to the purifying of the flesh: (V.14) How much more shall the blood of Christ, who through the eternal Spirit offered Himself without spot to God, purge your conscience from dead works to serve the living God?"

Verse twelve tells us "by His own blood He entered in once into the holy place, having obtained eternal redemption for us." This is the new covenant or the New Testament if you like. Jesus died once, and will never die again. He is what the Bible calls "the propitiation for our sins." The word "propitiation" means "appeasing," or "satisfying." God was satisfied with the sacrificial death of Jesus to atone for our sins. Hopefully these verses will explain it better than I can.

<u>ROMANS 3:25</u> - "Whom God hath set forth to be a propitiation through faith in His blood, to declare his righteousness for the remission of sins that are past, through the forbearance of God."

<u>**1 JOHN 2:2**</u> - "And He is the propitiation for our sins: and not for ours only, but also for the sins of the whole world."

<u>**1 JONN 4:10**</u> - "Herein is love, not that we loved God, but that He loved us, and sent His Son to be the propitiation for our sins."

A quick word about this new covenant:

<u>**HEBREWS 10:16-22**</u> - "This is the covenant that I will make with them after those days, saith the Lord, I will put My laws into their hearts, and in their minds will I write them; (V.17) And their sins and iniquities will I remember no more. (V.18) Now where remission of these is, there is no more offering for sin. (V.19) Having therefore, brethren, boldness to enter into the holiest by the blood of Jesus, (V.20) By a new and living way, which He hath consecrated for us, through the veil, that is to say, his flesh; (V.21) And having an high priest over the house of God; (V.22) Let us draw near with a true heart in full assurance of faith, having our hearts sprinkled from an evil conscience, and our bodies washed with pure water."

"Oh, the Blood of Jesus." "There's Power in the Blood." "Nothing but the Blood," and the list goes on. There's song after song about the blood of Jesus. I hope you have seen there would be no forgiveness of sin without the blood of Jesus. Hebrews 9:22b says: "without shedding of blood is no remission (*of sin*)." There truly is power in the blood of Jesus. If you want to get technical about it, this is what to believe for salvation. Jesus died (*shed His blood*). We believe this was done to atone for our sins. In believing so, we are "covered by the blood;" and because of this covering, we will have a home in heaven.

<u>REVELATION 7:14</u> - "And I said unto him, Sir, thou knowest. And he said to me, These are they which came out of great tribulation, and have washed their robes, and made them white in the blood of the Lamb."

<u>THE WORD</u>

Although Jesus has many names and titles, His proper name is Jesus. Joseph was told by the angel of the Lord His name shall be Jesus.

<u>MATTHEW 1:21</u> - "And she shall bring forth a son, and thou shalt call His name Jesus: for He shall save his people from their sins."

The following is a list of names and titles given specifically to our Lord Jesus. The more we study this list, the more we will understand who Jesus really is. All these names are taken from the King James Version of the Bible. (*In alphabetical order*)

ADAM, ADVOCATE
 ALMIGHTY
 ALPHA AND OMEGA
AMEN
APOSTLE OF OUR PROFESSION
ARM OF THE LORD
AUTHOR AND FINISHER OF OUR FAITH
AUTHOR OF ETERNAL SALVATION
BEGINNING OF CREATION OF GOD
BELOVED SON
BLESSED AND ONLY POTENTATE
BRANCH
BREAD OF LIFE
CAPTAIN OF SALVATION
CHIEF SHEPHERD
CHRIST OF GOD
CONSOLATION OF ISRAEL
CORNERSTONE
COUNSELLOR
CREATOR
DAYSPRING
DELIVERER
DESIRE OF THE NATIONS
DOOR

ELECT OF GOD
EVERLASTING FATHER
FAITHFUL WITNESS
FIRST AND LAST
FIRST BEGOTTEN
FORERUNNER
GLORY OF THE LORD
GOD
GOD BLESSED
GOOD SHEPHERD
GOVERNOR
GREAT HIGH PRIEST
HEAD OF THE CHURCH
HEIR OF ALL THINGS
HOLY CHILD
HOLY ONE
HOLY ONE OF GOD
HOLY ONE OF ISRAEL
HORN OF SALVATION
I AM
IMAGE OF GOD
IMMANUEL
JEHOVAH
JESUS OF NAZARETH
JUDGE OF ISRAEL
THE JUST ONE
KING
KING OF THE AGES
KING OF THE JEWS
KING OF KINGS
KING OF SAINTS

LAWGIVER
LAMB
LAMB OF GOD
LEADER AND COMMANDER
THE LIFE
LIGHT OF THE WORLD
LION OF THE TRIBE OF JUDAH
LORD OF ALL
LORD OF GLORY
LORD OF LORDS
LORD OF OUR RIGHTEOUSNESS
MAN OF SORROWS
MEDIATOR
MESSENGER OF THE COVENANT
MESSIAH
MIGHTY GOD
MIGHTY ONE
MORNING STAR
NAZARENE
ONLY BEGOTTEN SON
OUR PASSOVER
PRINCE OF LIFE
PRINCE OF KINGS
PRINCE OF PEACE
PROPHET
REDEEMER
RESURRECTION AND LIFE
ROCKROOT OF DAVID
ROSE OF SHARON
SAVIOR
SEED OF WOMAN

SHEPHERD AND BISHOP OF SOULS
SHILOH
SON OF THE BLESSED
SON OF DAVID
SON OF GOD
SON OF THE HIGHEST
SUN OF RIGHTEOUSNESS
TRUE LIGHT
TRUE VINE
TRUTH
WITNESS
WORD
WORD OF GOD

You could pick any one of these titles, and have an interesting Bible study searching the deep meanings of each one. However, as you can see by the title of his chapter, you know I just want to address the last two titles on this list. Jesus is called the Word, and the Word of God. I believe this is going to be a very interesting, and enlightening topic. I refer to my Bible as the Word of God. Inside the front cover of my Bible I wrote this quote: "This is my Bible, This is God speaking to me." I do understand that it is leather, paper, and ink, published by man, and written by man, but only under the inspiration of God (*2 Timothy 3:16 - "All scripture is given by inspiration of God."*); no other book can or does make a claim like that. I cherish my Bible. It truly is the Word of God. Bringing us to an interesting conclusion I came to;

since Jesus is The Word of God, and He is eternal; and since Matthew 24:35 tells us "Heaven and earth shall pass away, but My words (*The Word of God*) shall not pass away." Jesus, and the words contained in my Bible are one in the same. It is my belief that you will come to that same conclusion by the end of this chapter.

I understand the beginning is a good place to start, so let's just start at the beginning. The phrase "Word of God" is found forty four times in the New Testament. These next verses directly link that phrase to Jesus Christ Himself.

JOHN 1:1, 2 & 14 - "In the beginning was the Word (Jesus), and the Word was with God, and the Word was God. (V.2) The same was in the beginning with God. (V.14) And the Word (Jesus) was made flesh, and dwelt among us, (and we beheld his glory, the glory as of the only begotten of the Father,) full of grace and truth."

1 PETER 1:23 - "Being born again, not of corruptible seed, but of incorruptible, by the word of God, which liveth and abideth for ever."

1 JOHN 5:7 - "For there are three that bear record in heaven, the Father, the Word, and the Holy Ghost: and these three are one."

REVELATION 19:13 - "And He (*Jesus*) was clothed with a vesture dipped in blood: and His name is called The Word of God."

If you were to ask me the question of: why Jesus is called "The Word of God?" I would have to say "It's because He is." In the next section of this chapter we will look at reasons "because He is" is the correct response to the question of why Jesus is called "The Word of God." We will examine statements by or about Jesus in relation to His being The Word of God.

The first one we will look at is what is called "The Parable of the Sower." Here it is in case you are not familiar with how it goes. Pay particular attention the underlined section at the beginning of the parable; this will help you understand the verses to follow the parable

LUKE 8:5-8 - "A sower went out to sow his seed: and as he sowed, some fell by the way side; and it was trodden down, and the fowls of the air devoured it. (V.6) And some fell upon a rock; and as soon as it was sprung up, it withered away, because it lacked moisture. (V.7) And some fell among thorns; and the thorns sprang up with it, and choked it. (V.8) And other fell on good ground, and sprang up, and bare fruit an hundredfold. And when he had said these things, he cried, He that hath ears to hear let him hear."

Luke 8:9 tell us that His disciples asked him, "What might this parable be?" Next, is the start of how He explained it to them.

LUKE 8:11 &12 - "Now the parable is this: The seed is the word of God. (V.12) Those by the way side are they that hear; then cometh the devil, and taketh away the word out of their hearts, lest they should believe and be saved."

What He was telling them was that believing the Word is essential to our salvation. Just as we must believe in Jesus.

HEBREWS 11:6 - "But without faith it is impossible to please Him: for he that cometh to God must believe that He is, and that He is a rewarder of them that diligently seek Him."

EPHESIANS 2:8 - "For by grace are ye saved through faith; and that not of yourselves: it is the gift of God."

From those two verses alone you should see how important faith is to our salvation. Well then; how do we get this faith?

ROMANS 10:17 - "So then faith cometh by hearing, and hearing by the word of God."

Are you beginning to see that the word always comes back to the Word?

MATTHEW 24:9 - "Then shall they deliver you up to be afflicted, and shall kill you: and ye shall be hated of all nations <u>for my name's sake</u>."

REVELATION 6:9 - "And when he had opened the fifth seal, I saw under the altar the souls of them that were slain <u>for the word of God</u>, and for the testimony which they held."

The word of God is crucial and essential to the creating and maintaining of the universe. Most all of us are familiar with the verse "and God said let there be light: And there was light (*Genesis 1:3*)." However, most are unaware of the magnitude of that verse. God <u>spoke</u> the world into existence. He put everything in its proper place, so that it all works in harmony with each other, by His word.

HEBREWS 11:13 - "Through faith we understand that the worlds were framed by the <u>word of God</u>, so that things which are seen were not made of things which do appear."

I want to really get deep with these next verses. Since God spoke the world into existence. Would you conclude with me that by the word of God this world was made? John makes it abundantly clear that God and Jesus are the same yet different (*see The Trinity*).So, if the word of God is responsible for all that we see. Jesus actually formed it. In the following verses; three is referring to Jesus. If I may paraphrase, it basically says if Jesus didn't make it, it was not made! Read the following verses if you are not convinced.

JOHN 1:1-3 - "In the beginning was the Word, and the Word was with God, and the Word was God. (V.2) The same was in the beginning with God. (V.3) All things were made by Him (*Jesus*); and without Him was not any thing made that was made."

COLOSSIANS 1:15-17 - "(*Jesus*) Who is the image of the invisible God, the firstborn of every creature: (V.16) For by Him were all things created, that are in heaven, and that are in earth, visible and invisible, whether they be thrones, or dominions, or principalities, or powers: all things were created by Him, and for Him*(V.17) And He is before all things, and by Him all things consist."

HEBREWS 1:2 - "Hath in these last days spoken unto us by his Son, whom He hath appointed heir of all things, by whom also He made the worlds."

***REVELATION 4:11** - "Thou art worthy, O Lord, to receive glory and honour and power: for thou hast created all things, and for thy pleasure they are and were created."

The Word Must Abide in You

JOHN15:4 - "Abide in me, and I in you. As the branch cannot bear fruit of itself, except it abide in the vine; no more can ye, except ye abide in me."

COLOSSIANS 3:16 - "Let the word of Christ dwell in you richly in all wisdom; teaching and admonishing one another in psalms and hymns and spiritual songs, singing with grace in your hearts to the Lord."

1 JOHN 2:14 - "I have written unto you, fathers, because ye have known him that is from the beginning. I have written unto you, young men, because ye are strong, and the word of God abideth in you, and ye have overcome the wicked one."

THE SWORD

EPHESIANS 6:17 - "And take the helmet of salvation, and the sword of the Spirit, which is the word of God."

HEBREWS 4:12 - "For the word of God is quick, and powerful, and sharper than any twoedged sword, piercing even to the dividing asunder of soul and spirit, and of the joints and marrow, and is a discerner of the thoughts and intents of the heart."

REVELATION 1:16 - "And He (*Jesus*) had in

his right hand seven stars: and out of his mouth went a sharp twoedged sword: and his countenance was as the sun shineth in his strength."

<u>REVELATION 19:15</u> - "And out of His (*Jesus*) mouth goeth a sharp sword, that with it He should smite the nations: and He shall rule them with a rod of iron: and He treadeth the winepress of the fierceness and wrath of Almighty God."

I hope that you have been enlightened about who and what the Word of God is. I want to one last thought before I close this section. I mentioned this verse at the beginning of this chapter, let's look at it again.

<u>2 TIMOTHY 3:16</u> - "All scripture (*the Word of God*) is given by inspiration of God, and is profitable for doctrine, for reproof, for correction, for instruction in righteousness"

Sure, men wrote the Bible. It had to be put on paper somehow; and it's not that God couldn't have done it. The words contained in the Bible are the words of God. These men were "inspired by God" to write down what He gave them (*2 PETER 1:20 &21- "Knowing this first, that no prophecy of the scripture is of any private interpretation. (V.21) For the prophecy came not in old time by the will of man: but holy men of God spake as they were moved by the Holy Ghost."*). I liken it to a secretary taking dictation for their boss. They write down exactly what they say. Nothing else is added, their own thoughts aren't injected, and it's just what the boss says. The letter or memo represents his thoughts and his character. That's why there is this warning at the end of the book of Revelation.

<u>REVELATION 22:18&19</u> - "For I testify unto every man that heareth the words of the prophecy of this book, If any man shall add unto these things, God shall add unto him the plagues that are written in this book: (V.19) And if any man shall take away from the words of the book of this prophecy, God shall take away his part out of the book of life, and out of the holy city, and from the things which are written in this book."

This was Jesus who said these things. Truly He is The Word of God!

THE NAME OF JESUS

Have you ever been a name dropper? You know, using someone else's name to grant you favor or access to something or someone; it is used a mostly to acquire a job. Another use of this word is used by insecure people who feel the need to impress others by mentioning an important person they claim to know. Name dropping is not a good practice to get into especially if the person didn't give you permission to use their name. I'm so glad that Jesus gave me permission to use His name. In fact He told us to use His name when we pray.

JOHN 14:13 - "And whatsoever ye shall ask in my name, that will I do, that the Father may be glorified in the Son."

JOHN 14:14 - "If ye shall ask any thing in my name, I will do it."

JOHN 16:23 - "And in that day ye shall ask me nothing. Verily, verily, I say unto you, Whatsoever ye shall ask the Father in my name, He will give it you."

JOHN 16:26 - "At that day ye shall ask in my name: and I say not unto you, that I will pray the Father for you."

Peter must have been listening when Jesus

said this, and decided to put it into action. Acts three tells us that as Peter and John were walking up to the temple together. They saw a lame man by the gate of the temple asking for alms. "Then Peter said, Silver and gold have I none; but such as I have give I thee: In the name of Jesus Christ of Nazareth rise up and walk (V.6)." In verse eight we find the man healed walking, and leaping, and praising God as he entered with them into the temple. What happened next is hard to believe. A time of rejoicing turned into a time of questioning, and trial. Even though Peter told them in Acts 3:16: "And His name (Jesus) through faith in His name hath made this man strong, whom ye see and know: yea, the faith which is by him hath given him this perfect soundness in the presence of you all. The priests, and the captain of the temple, and the Sadducees, took them and put them in jail until the next day. Then they were brought out and placed in the midst of Annas the high priest, Caiaphas, the rulers, elders, and scribes; here is what took place next.

<u>ACTS 4:7-10, 18</u>- "And when they had set them in the midst, they asked, By what power, or by what name, have ye done this? (V.8) Then Peter, filled with the Holy Ghost, said unto them, Ye rulers of the people, and elders of Israel, (V.9) If we this day be examined of the good deed done to the impotent man, by what means he is made whole; (V.10) Be it known unto you all, and to all

the people of Israel, that <u>by the name of Jesus Christ of Nazareth,</u> whom ye crucified, whom God raised from the dead, even by Him doth this man stand here before you whole. (V.18) And they called them, and commanded them not to speak at all nor teach in the name of Jesus."

From that account of a miraculous healing, we can clearly see that there is power in the name of Jesus. This may be why God gave us the Third Commandment "Thou shalt not take the name of the LORD thy God in vain; for the LORD will not hold him guiltless that taketh his name (*Exodus 20:7*)." Paul wrote to the Philippians about the prominence (*importance*) of the name of Jesus.

<u>PHILIPPIANS 2:9-11</u> - "Wherefore God also hath highly exalted him, and given him a name which is above every name. (V.10) That at the name of Jesus every knee should bow, of things in heaven, and things in earth, and things under the earth; (V.11) And that every tongue should confess that Jesus Christ is Lord, to the glory of God the Father.

His name is so important it is the most essential part of our salvation.

<u>JOHN 14:6</u> - "Jesus saith unto him, I am the way, the truth, and the life: no man cometh unto the Father, but by me."

JOHN 20:31 - "But these are written, that ye might believe that Jesus is the Christ, the Son of God; and that believing ye might have life through his name."

ACTS 2:38 - "Then Peter said unto them, Repent, and be baptized every one of you in the name of Jesus Christ for the remission of sins, and ye shall receive the gift of the Holy Ghost."

ACTS 4:12- "Neither is there salvation in any other: for there is none other name under heaven given among men, whereby we must be saved."

ROMANS 10:9&10 - "That if thou shalt confess with thy mouth the Lord Jesus, and shalt believe in thine heart that God hath raised him from the dead, thou shalt be saved. (V.10) For with the heart man believeth unto righteousness; and with the mouth confession is made unto salvation."

It is a comfort to know

ROMANS 10:13 - "For whosoever shall call upon the name of the Lord shall be saved."

Remember how Jesus said "whatsoever ye shall ask in my name" I will do it. He meant it when He said "whosoever." In this following verse Jesus tells us that if we believe. We can do the same things He did, and even greater things than those that He did! The key though is to ask in His name.

JOHN 14:12&13 - "Verily, verily, I say unto you, He that believeth on me, the works that I do shall he do also; and greater works than these shall he do; because I go unto my Father. (V.13) And whatsoever ye shall ask in my name, that will I do, that the Father may be glorified in the Son."

One of the things He did was to cast out evil spirits from those who were possessed by them.
MATTHEW 8:16 - "When the even was come, they brought unto Him many that were possessed with devils: and He cast out the spirits with His word, and healed all that were sick."

Below are three accounts of casting out demons using the name of Jesus. I guess you could say there is a right way and a wrong way to go about doing this.

LUKE 10:17 - "And the seventy returned again with joy, saying, Lord, even the devils are subject unto us through thy name."

ACTS 16:18 -"And this did she many days. But Paul, being grieved, turned and said to the spirit, I command thee in the name of Jesus Christ to come out of her. And he came out the same hour."
ACTS 19:13-16 - "Then certain of the

vagabond Jews, exorcists, took upon them to call over them which had evil spirits the name of the Lord Jesus, saying, We adjure you by Jesus whom Paul preacheth. (V.14) And there were seven sons of one Sceva, a Jew, and chief of the priests, which did so. (V.15) And the evil spirit answered and said, Jesus I know, and Paul I know; but who are ye? (V.16) And the man in whom the evil spirit was leaped on them, and overcame them, and prevailed against them, so that they fled out of that house naked and wounded."

I've mentioned earlier how important the name of Jesus is to us. That name has so much power. We might forget to use it in our everyday activities. Below are few verses that need to be on our refrigerators, and our hearts.

EPHESIANS 5:20 -"Giving thanks always for all things unto God and the Father in the name of our Lord Jesus Christ."

COLOSSIANS 3:17 &23 -"And whatsoever ye do in word or deed, do all in the name of the Lord Jesus, giving thanks to God and the Father by him. (V.23) And whatsoever ye do, do it heartily, as to the Lord, and not unto men."

There are many more scripture verses with the term "the name of our Lord Jesus Christ" in them. I believe what is in this chapter is more than enough information to make anyone aware of the power behind the name of Jesus. This is a name to live for, and a name to die for.

ACTS 15:26 - "Men that have hazarded their lives for the name of our Lord Jesus Christ."

ACTS 21:13 - "Then Paul answered, What mean ye to weep and to break mine heart? for I am ready not to be bound only, but also to die at Jerusalem <u>for the name of the Lord Jesus</u>."

<u>WAS (IS) JESUS THE MESSIAH?</u>

The question of Jesus being the long awaited Messiah is still debated to this very day. The Bible provides us with more than enough proof that He is indeed He who was promised to come. However, there are still those who will not believe it. Here are just a couple examples of this happening.

JOHN 1:11 - "He came unto his own, and his own received him not."

LUKE 13:34 - "O Jerusalem, Jerusalem, which killest the prophets, and stonest them that are sent unto thee; how often would I have gathered thy children together, as a hen doth gather her brood under her wings, and ye would not!"

The Bible also tells us time and time again that He was "the stone the builders rejected," but that's not enough. Let's just forget about the 456 Messianic prophecies. How do we know? How can we tell?

I suggest we look at His name. There is a lot to be said about a name. The angel of the Lord told Joseph "thou shalt call his name JESUS." However, He is called Jesus Christ one hundred and ninety three times in the New Testament. The title "Christ" is the most frequently used title for Jesus in the New Testament. Jesus is His name; "Christ (*Christos*)" is a title that actually means "Messiah, the Son of God."

Was He the Messiah? If there was any one person at that time who should know it would have been His cousin, John the Baptist. John knew who Jesus was while they were both in their mothers' wombs. Mary (*Jesus' mother*) went to visit her cousin Elisabeth (*Johns' mother*) while they were both still pregnant. Luke wrote that when Mary entered the house and called for Elisabeth. John "leaped in her womb."

LUKE 1:40-44 - "And entered into the house of Zacharias, and saluted Elisabeth. (V.41) And it came to pass, that, when Elisabeth heard the salutation of Mary, the babe leaped in her womb; and Elisabeth was filled with the Holy Ghost. (V.42) And she spake out with a loud voice, and said, Blessed art thou among women, and blessed is the fruit of thy womb. (V.43) And whence is this to me, that the mother of my Lord should come to me? (V.44) For, lo, as soon as the voice of thy salutation sounded in mine ears, the babe leaped in my womb for joy."

Obviously, since Elisabeth was filled with the Holy Ghost, she knew who this baby was that Mary was carrying. How did John know who Jesus was? Luke 1:15 tells us that "he shall be filled with the Holy Ghost, even from his mother's womb." In fact Elisabeth, her husband Zacharias, and their baby (*John*) were the first people in the new testament to be filled with the Holy Ghost (*Luke 1:15, 41 & 67*).

Yes, John knew who Jesus was, and more importantly, he knew who he was.

<u>JOHN 1:19-23</u> - "And this is the record of John, when the Jews sent priests and Levites from Jerusalem to ask him (*John the Baptist*), Who art thou? (V.20) And he confessed, and denied not; but confessed, I am not the Christ. (V.21) And they asked him, What then? Art thou Elias? And he saith, I am not. Art thou that prophet? And he answered, No (V.22) Then said they unto him, Who art thou? that we may give an answer to them that sent us. What sayest thou of thyself? (V.23) He said, I am the voice of one crying in the wilderness, Make straight the way of the Lord, as said the prophet Esaias."

As I've mentioned, John the Baptist was keenly aware of who Jesus was. This was evident by the remarks he made on a certain day when he was baptizing in the Jordan River. When he saw Jesus coming to be baptized he said.

JOHN 1:29, 24, 36 - "The next day John seeth Jesus coming unto him, and saith, Behold the Lamb of God, which taketh away the sin of the world. (V.34) And I saw, and bare record that this is the Son of God. (V.36) And looking upon Jesus as He walked, he saith, Behold the Lamb of God!"

After making definitive statements such as those, and being filled with the Holy Ghost. You should have no question about who Jesus was; right? Well, life happens, and sometimes we can question things we were once so sure of. Such was the case with John the Baptist. He preached the truth about Herod, telling him it was not lawful for him to have his brother's wife Herodias, as his wife. Mark 6:17 tells what happened next: "For Herod himself had sent forth and laid hold upon John, and bound him in prison for Herodias' sake, his brother Philip's wife: for he had married her." So here we have John in jail waiting for his cousin the Messiah to come get him out. Is that a fair enough assumption? Jesus doesn't come and apparently does nothing about John's situation. I'm not sure why He didn't intervene; after all John was beheaded because of an oath he made to his wife's daughter Salome. But, before he was beheaded, John was questioning who Jesus was.

MATTHEW 11:2-5 - "Now when John had heard in the prison the works of Christ, he sent two of his disciples, (V.3) And said unto him, Art thou He that should come, or do we look for another? (V.4) Jesus answered and said unto them, Go and show John again those things which ye do hear and see: (V.5) The blind receive their sight, and the lame walk, the lepers are cleansed, and the deaf hear, the dead are raised up, and the poor have the gospel preached to them."

Some may say that Jesus really didn't answer the question they were asking. I believe He answered them perfectly. The blind receiving their sight, the lame walking, the lepers cleansed, the deaf hearing, the dead being raised up, and the poor having the gospel preached to them, are all things prophesized that the Messiah would do. ("Jesus answered them, I told you, and ye believed not: the works that I do in my Father's name, they bear witness of me - John 10:25").I think John knew what the scriptures said about the Messiah, and was satisfied with what Jesus told these men to tell him.

Did Jesus ever admit that He was the Messiah? Jesus did not want to let very many people know that He was the promised Christ. Throughout His ministry, Jesus was very guarded about who would know that He was the Messiah. Jesus kept His identity hidden so that He would not encourage incomplete expectations of Him and bring upon Himself the wrath of the Roman government before His appointed time.

MARK 3:9-12 - "And He spake to his disciples, that a small ship should wait on Him because of the multitude, lest they should throng him. (V.10) For He had healed many; insomuch that they pressed upon Him for to touch Him, as many as had plagues. (V.11) And unclean spirits, when they saw Him, fell down before Him, and cried, saying, Thou art the Son of God. (V.12) And He straitly charged them that they should not make him known."

MARK 5:41-43 - "And He took the damsel by the hand, and said unto her, Talitha cumi; which is, being interpreted, Damsel, I say unto thee, arise. (V.42) And straightway the damsel arose, and walked; for she was of the age of twelve years. And they were astonished with a great astonishment. (V.43) And He charged them straitly that no man should know it; and commanded that something should be given her to eat."

MARK 8:29&30 - "And He saith unto them, But whom say ye that I am? And Peter answereth and saith unto Him, Thou art the Christ. (V.30) And He charged them that they should tell no man of Him."

Jesus instructed those mentioned above not to mention that He was the Christ. They knew who He was. But, how about those who were unsure and straightly asked Him who He was? Jesus didn't deny that He was the Messiah.

MATTHEW 27:11 - "And Jesus stood before the governor (*Pontius Pilate*): and the governor asked Him, saying, Art thou the King of the Jews? And Jesus said unto him, Thou sayest."

LUKE 22:67-71 - "Art thou the Christ? tell us. And He said unto them, If I tell you, ye will not believe: (V.68) And if I also ask you, ye will not answer me, nor let me go. (V.69) Hereafter shall the Son of man sit on the right hand of the power of God. (V.70) Then said they all, Art thou then the Son of God? And He said unto them, Ye say that I am. (V.71) And they said, What need we any further witness? for we ourselves have heard of his own mouth."

MARK 14:60-63 - "And the high priest stood up in the midst, and asked Jesus, saying,

Answerest thou nothing? what is it which these witness against thee? (V.61) But he held his peace, and answered nothing. Again the high priest asked him, and said unto him, Art thou the Christ, the Son of the Blessed? (V.62) And Jesus said, I am: and ye shall see the Son of man sitting on the right hand of power, and coming in the clouds of heaven. (V.63) Then the high priest rent his clothes, and saith, What need we any further witnesses?"

I need to point out that there are no contradictions in these verses. When Jesus told Pontius Pilate "Thou sayest," and to the priests "Ye say that I am." He was actually saying "It is as thou hast said." Therefore admitting that He is the Son of God. Mark states that Jesus plainly said "I am" to the question of His deity. This is where the high priest tore his clothes, and in both cases said; "What need we any further witness?"

He didn't mince words when He had the infamous conversation with the Samaritan woman at the well. Jesus told her exactly who He was!

JOHN 4:25 &26 - "The (*Samaritan*) woman saith unto Him, I know that Messias cometh, which is called Christ: when He is come, He will tell us all things. (V.26) Jesus saith unto her, I that speak unto thee am He."

JOHN 4:28 &29 - "The woman then left her waterpot, and went her way into the city, and saith to the men, (V.29) Come, see a man, which told me all things that ever I did: is not this the Christ?"

Is Jesus the promised Messiah? The people who attended His triumphant entry into Jerusalem thought so; or did they? Is He the Messiah, or a prophet? I hope this study will help you to answer correctly when you are asked "Who is this? He is "He that cometh in the name of the Lord; Hosanna in the highest."

MATTHEW 21:9-11 "And the multitudes that went before, and that followed, cried, saying, Hosanna to the son of David: Blessed is He that cometh in the name of the Lord; Hosanna in the highest. (V.10) And when He was come into Jerusalem, all the city was moved, saying, Who is this? (V.11) And the multitude said, This is Jesus the prophet of Nazareth of Galilee."

THE PRAYERS OF JESUS

You may think that Jesus would have no need to pray since He was God in flesh. The flesh part is why He prayed. We are told that there were times when He'd spend many hours in prayer, there was even times when Jesus prayed all night.

MARK 1:35 - "And in the morning, rising up a great while before day, He went out, and departed into a solitary place, and there prayed."

MARK 6:46 - "And when He had sent them away, He departed into a mountain to pray."

LUKE 6:12 - "And it came to pass in those days, that He went out into a mountain to pray, and continued all night in prayer to God."

If you'll look again at these three verses. You will see a reoccurring word in each one, "He". These verses are in reference to the private prayer life of Jesus. When He was alone with His Father, it seems Jesus would tend to take a long time with His prayers. However, His public prayer life was quite different. It may surprise you to know that Jesus didn't pray long prayers in public. The following verses are examples of prayers Jesus prayed when He was out among the people. I want you to pay particular attention to the bold underlined words, these are the actual prayers.

MATTHEW 8:3 - "And Jesus put forth his hand, and touched him, saying, I will; be thou clean. And immediately his leprosy was cleansed."

MATTHEW 8:8,13 - "The centurion answered

and said, Lord, I am not worthy that thou shouldest come under my roof: but speak the word only, and my servant shall be healed. (V.13) And Jesus said unto the centurion, Go thy way; and as thou hast believed, so be it done unto thee. And his servant was healed in the selfsame hour."

MATTHEW 9:21-22 - "For she said within herself, If I may but touch His garment, I shall be whole. (V.22) But Jesus turned him about, and when He saw her, He said, Daughter, be of good comfort; thy faith hath made thee whole. And the woman was made whole from that hour."

MATTHWE 9:28-29 -"And when he was come into the house, the blind men came to him: and Jesus saith unto them, Believe ye that I am able to do this? They said unto him, Yea, Lord. (V.29) Then touched he their eyes, saying, According to your faith be it unto you."

MATTHEW 12:10-13 - "And, behold, there was a man which had his hand withered. And they asked him, saying, Is it lawful to heal on the sabbath days? (V.12) Wherefore it is lawful to do well on the sabbath days. (V.13) Then saith He to the man, Stretch forth thine hand. And he stretched it forth; and it was restored whole, like as the other."

MARK 4:39 - "And he arose, and rebuked the

wind, and said unto the sea, Peace, be still. And the wind ceased, and there was a great calm."

MARK 5:41-42 - "And he took the damsel by the hand, and said unto her, Talitha cumi; which is, being interpreted, Damsel, I say unto thee, arise. (V.42) And straightway the damsel arose"

MARK 10:52 - "And Jesus said unto him, Go thy way; thy faith hath made thee whole. And immediately he received his sight, and followed Jesus in the way."

MARK 7:32-35 - "And they bring unto him one that was deaf, and had an impediment in his speech; and they beseech Him to put His hand upon him. (V. 33) And He took him aside from the multitude, and put His fingers into his ears, and He spit, and touched his tongue; (V.34) And looking up to heaven, he sighed, and saith unto him, Ephphatha, that is, Be opened. (V.35) And straightway his ears were opened, and the string of his tongue was loosed, and he spake plain."

LUKE 7:13 - "And when the Lord saw her, He had compassion on her, and said unto her, Weep not. (V.14) And He came and touched the bier: and they that bare him stood still. And he said, Young man, I say unto thee, Arise. (V.15) And he that was dead sat up"

LUKE 17:12&14, 17-19 - "And as He entered into a certain village, there met him ten men that were lepers, (V.14) And when He saw them, He said unto them, Go show yourselves unto the priests. And it came to pass, that, as they went, they were cleansed. (V.17) And Jesus answering said, Were there not ten cleansed? but where are the nine? (V.18) There are not found that returned to give glory to God, save this stranger. (V.19) And He said unto him, Arise, go thy way: thy faith hath made thee whole."

LUKE 18:41-43 - "Saying, What wilt thou that I shall do unto thee? And he said, Lord, that I may receive my sight. (V.42) And Jesus said unto him, Receive thy sight: thy faith hath saved thee. (V. 43) And immediately he received his sight, and followed him, glorifying God: and all the people, when they saw it, gave praise unto God."

JOHN 2:5-8 - "His mother saith unto the servants, Whatsoever He saith unto you, do it. (V. 6) And there were set there six waterpots of stone, after the manner of the purifying of the Jews, containing two or three firkins apiece. (V. 7) Jesus saith unto them, Fill the waterpots with water. And they filled them up to the brim. (V.8) And He saith unto them, Draw out now, and bear unto the governor of the feast. And they bare it."

JOHN 5:5, 6, 8 & 9 - "And a certain man was

there, which had an infirmity thirty and eight years. (V.6) When Jesus saw him lie, and knew that he had been now a long time in that case, he saith unto him, Wilt thou be made whole? (V.8) Jesus saith unto him, Rise, take up thy bed, and walk. (V.9) And immediately the man was made whole, and took up his bed, and walked:"

JOHN 11:41-44 - "Then they took away the stone from the place where the dead was laid. And Jesus lifted up His eyes, and said, Father, I thank thee that thou hast heard me. (V.42) And I knew that thou hearest me always: but because of the people which stand by I said it, that they may believe that thou hast sent me. (V.43) And when he thus had spoken, he cried with a loud voice, Lazarus, come forth. (V.44) And he that was dead came forth"

You probably didn't realize how short the prayers of Jesus were. You probably also didn't realize most of the time He told the people "thy faith hath made thee whole." When we come to Jesus it takes faith. So, Jesus didn't pray long public prayers. Matthew 6:7 tells us that Jesus warned against this, when He said "But when ye pray, use not vain repetitions, as the heathen do: for they think that they shall be heard for their much speaking." The longest recorded prayer of Jesus is John seventeen (*the entire chapter*). Notice that I said "recorded." Because of course there were many times Jesus prayed, but the Bible doesn't tell us how long they were.

Probably one of the better known prayers of Jesus was when He prayed in the garden before He was betrayed. We will look at this account from the books of Matthew and Luke.

MATTHEW 26:36-44 - "Then cometh Jesus with them unto a place called Gethsemane, and saith unto the disciples, Sit ye here, while I go and pray yonder. (V.37) And He took with Him Peter and the two sons of Zebedee, and began to be sorrowful and very heavy. (V.38) Then saith He unto them, My soul is exceeding sorrowful, even unto death: tarry

ye here, and watch with me. (V.39) And He went a little farther, and fell on His face, and prayed, saying, O my Father, if it be possible, let this cup pass from me: nevertheless not as I will, but as thou wilt. (V.40) And He cometh unto the disciples, and findeth them asleep, and saith unto Peter, What, could ye not watch with me one hour? (V.41) Watch and pray, that ye enter not into temptation: the spirit indeed is willing, but the flesh is weak. (V.42) He went away again the second time, and prayed, saying, O my Father, if this cup may not pass away from me, except I drink it, thy will be done. (V.43) And He came and found them asleep again: for their eyes were heavy. (V.44) And He left them, and went away again, and prayed the third time, saying the same words."

LUKE22:40-44 - "And when He was at the place, He said unto them, Pray that ye enter not into temptation. (V.41) And He was withdrawn from them about a stone's cast, and kneeled down, and prayed, (V.42) Saying, Father, if thou be willing, remove this cup from me: nevertheless not my will, but thine, be done. (V.43) And there appeared an angel unto Him from heaven, strengthening Him. (V.44) And being in an agony He prayed more earnestly: and His sweat was as it were great drops of blood falling down to the ground."

Don't get me wrong: I do understand that Jesus was about to take the sins of all mankind upon Him. But this was one time that His being in flesh prompted Him to pray. Let's look at this I depth. First, make no mistake about it, this was a physical battle not only a spiritual one. Jesus was willing to die for our sins. That's why He was sent. When Jesus stated in Mark 14:38 "Watch ye and pray, lest ye enter into temptation. The spirit truly is ready, but the flesh is weak," He could have easily been talking about Himself too. Jesus knew what was going to happen to Him, and quite frankly wasn't looking forward to it. He prayed that His father would take this cup away. You could say He approached God and asked if there was any other way it could be played out (*Mark*

14:36: "And He said, Abba, Father, all things are possible unto thee; take away this cup from me").

Let's look at this play by play. He brought some of His disciples with Him. Was it for comfort, moral support, or something else? Now the strange thing is He didn't say "hey let's a prayer meeting." He didn't ask them to pray for Him. He told them to pray for themselves. Then "He went a little farther" and prayed by Himself (*sometimes you just want to be alone*). His prayer was basically to have "this cup" removed. The cup was the suffering He would endure. He was already feeling the effects of it. We are told He was exceeding sorrowful and very heavy. He was in agony, "and His sweat was as it were great drops of blood falling down to the ground." This is called Hematidrosis, and it is real, but a very rare, medical condition; its cause is extreme anguish. A little known fact is that God sent an angel unto Him from heaven, to strengthening Him. He didn't remove the cup; even though Jesus prayed the same prayer three times, but He helped Jesus to complete His task. It didn't help any to find His disciples sleeping either, but He prayed until the hour of his betrayal had come.

THE LORD"S PRAYER?

MATTHEW 6:9-13 - *"After this manner therefore pray ye: Our Father which art in heaven, Hallowed be thy name. (V. 10) Thy kingdom come.*

Thy will be done in Earth, as it is in heaven. (V. 11) Give us this day our daily bread. (V. 12) And forgive us our debts, as we forgive our debtors. (V. 13) And lead us not into temptation, but deliver us from evil: For thine is the kingdom, and the power, and the glory, for ever. Amen."

I mentioned above that probably one of the better known prayers of Jesus was when He prayed in the garden. However, the most well known prayer the Lord gave us isn't even a prayer. If you haven't guessed I'm speaking of the "Lord's Prayer." In the book of Luke he tells us; "And it came to pass, that, as He was praying in a certain place, when He ceased, one of his disciples said unto Him, Lord, teach us to pray, as John also taught his disciples (*Luke 11:1*)." Jesus' response to him was "<u>After this manner</u> therefore pray ye… (*Matthew 6:9-13*)." He never said this was a prayer, and He never prayed it. What He was telling them was; this is how you are to pray. He said to pray in this manner. I don't know why this is named the Lord's Prayer. The Lord's Prayer is actually found in the book of John, chapter seventeen (*the whole chapter*). Jesus couldn't have prayed this because in Luke 11:4 the word "sin" was used instead of "debt" that is used here in verse twelve. Since Jesus never sinned. He wouldn't have prayed this, meaning it could not be the Lord's prayer! Yet many people recite it often, always as a prayer. Don't get me wrong. It's a great model of what and how we need to pray.

Jesus is our example for many things. One of those things is to give thanks for the food we receive. As we read above. Jesus taught us to pray.

MATTHEW 6:11 - "Give us this day our daily bread."

This made me think of an interesting point. When He was in the wilderness being tempted, we are told.

MATTHEW 4:3 - "And when the tempter came to Him, he said, If thou be the Son of God, command that these stones be made bread."

Now the point is; I believe He is the Son of God, and could "command that these stones be made bread." Nothing is impossible with God. Do you remember when the multitude followed Jesus and His disciples out to a "desert place" and had nothing to eat?

MARK 6:41&42 - "And when He had taken the five loaves and the two fishes, He looked up to heaven, and blessed, and brake the loaves, and gave them to His disciples to set before them; and the two fishes divided he among them all. (V.42) And they did all eat, and were filled."

Jesus, "the Bread of Life" who can make

bread appear, still takes time to ask a blessing over it. This is a good example for us to follow.

MATTHEW 26:26 - "And as they were eating, Jesus took bread, and blessed it, and brake it, and gave it to the disciples, and said, Take, eat; this is my body."

JOHN 20:30 &31- "And many other signs truly did Jesus in the presence of His disciples, which are not written in this book: (V.31) But these are written, that ye might believe that Jesus is the Christ, the Son of God; and that believing ye might have life through His name."

THE CONTROVERSIAL JESUS

People have no problem believing in God or that there is a God; but Jesus is another story. The Jewish people in Jesus' day wholly believed in God the Father, but couldn't believe that Jesus was the promised Messiah. This is made clear to us by the fact that Jesus was repeatedly accused as being a blasphemer. You have to believe in a holy God, to commit blaspheme against Him. This is also why He was often referred to as "the stone the builders rejected" in the scriptures. This is so evident in the story of the healing of the lame man in Acts three and four. After it was all said and done, the Peter and John were told (*"commanded"*) not to speak at all nor teach in the name of Jesus (*Acts 4:18*). They were not told to stop teaching, speaking, or I imagine even praying; just not to do it in the name of Jesus. This still goes on even to this very day. There could be a conversation about religious matters, and everything is okay. Then someone brings up Jesus, and the people talking get all tensed up; as if He is a forbidden subject. It's sad to say that in some cultures to mention the name Jesus is against the law. This is a very serious offence against the Father. John the apostle wrote about this in his first letter to what is termed as "The "Johannine Community." This was a community of people who were inspired by his teachings. They were located somewhere in southern Palestine; and warned them against this offence.

<u>1 JOHN 2:22&23</u> - "Who is a liar but he that denieth that Jesus is the Christ? He is antichrist, that denieth the Father and the Son. (V.23) Whosoever denieth the Son, the same hath not the Father: (but) he that acknowledgeth the Son hath the Father also."

<u>1 JOHN 4:2 &3</u>- "Hereby know ye the Spirit of God: Every spirit that confesseth that Jesus Christ is come in the flesh is of God: (V.3) And every spirit that confesseth not that Jesus Christ is come in the flesh is not of God: and this is that spirit of antichrist, whereof ye have heard that it should come; and even now already is it in the world."

1 JOHN 4:15 -"Whosoever shall confess that Jesus is the Son of God, God dwelleth in him, and he in God."

The birth of Jesus changed everything. It was already mentioned about how His birth caused our dates to be known as B.C and AD. This major change in history had, has, nor ever will be repeated again. Jesus said and did things that were very controversial. That's why I believe the title of this chapter is a good way to describe Him. The definition of the word "controversial" is "that it is argument causing: provoking, strong disagreement or disapproval, e.g. in public debate." One of my favorite verses shares this sentiment (*feeling*).

MARK 2:12- "And immediately he arose, took up the bed, and went forth before them all; insomuch that they were all amazed, and glorified God, saying, We never saw it on this fashion. (*in this manner, thus, so*)

Jesus said and did things that people had never seen or heard. He was so different from "the norm," people just didn't understand where He was coming from. In the verses below we see how this lack of understanding almost got Him stoned and also about how some people stopped following Him because of what He said.

JOHN 8:56-59- "Your father Abraham rejoiced to see my day: and he saw it, and was glad. (V.57) Then said the Jews unto Him, Thou art not yet fifty years old, and hast thou seen Abraham? (V.58) Jesus said unto them, Verily, verily, I say unto you, Before Abraham was, I am. (V.59) Then took they up stones to cast at him: but Jesus hid himself, and went out of the temple, going through the midst of them, and so passed by."

JOHN 6:51-66- "I am the living bread which came down from heaven: if any man eat of this bread, he shall live for ever: and the bread that I will give is my flesh, which I will give for the life of the world. (V.52) The Jews therefore strove among themselves, saying, How can this man give us his flesh to eat? (V.53) Then Jesus said unto them, Verily, verily, I say unto you, Except ye eat the flesh of the Son of man, and drink his blood, ye have no life in you. (V.54) Whoso eateth my flesh, and drinketh my blood, hath eternal life; and I will raise him up at the last day. (V.55) For my flesh is meat indeed, and my blood is drink indeed. (V.56) He that eateth my flesh, and drinketh my blood, dwelleth in me, and I in him. (V.57) As the living Father hath sent me, and I live by the Father: so he that eateth me, even he shall live by me. (V.58) This is that bread which came down from heaven: not as your fathers did eat manna, and are dead: he that eateth of this bread shall live for ever. (V.59) These things said he in the synagogue, as he taught in Capernaum. (V.60) Many therefore of his disciples, when they had heard this, said, This is an hard saying; who can hear it? (V.61) When Jesus knew in himself that his disciples murmured at it, he said unto them, Doth this offend you? (V.62) What and if ye shall see the Son of man ascend up where he was before? (V.63) It is the spirit that quickeneth; the flesh profiteth nothing: the words that I speak unto you, they are spirit, and they are life. (V.64) But there are some of you that believe not. For Jesus knew from the beginning who they were that believed not, and who should betray Him. (V.65) And He said, Therefore said I unto you, that no man can come unto me, except it were given unto him of my Father. (V.66) From that time many of His disciples went back, and walked no more with Him."

<u>PRINCE OF PEACE?</u>

When Isaiah prophesied of the coming Messiah he wrote: " For unto us a child is born, unto us a son is given: and the government shall be upon His shoulder: and His name shall be called Wonderful, Counsellor, The mighty God, The everlasting Father, The Prince of Peace (*Isaiah*

9:6)." I'd like us to look at the last title given to Him; The Prince of Peace. Jesus is this "Prince of Peace. As a King, He preserves the peace, commands peace, and creates peace, in His kingdom. He is our peace, and it is His peace that both keeps the hearts of his people and rules in them. In John 14:27Jesus told His disciples; "Peace I leave with you, my peace I give unto you: not as the world giveth, give I unto you. Let not your heart be troubled, neither let it be afraid." Jesus is The Prince of Peace, but not as we know peace. Jesus wants to give us an inner peace. Paul said it best in his letter to the Philippians where he wrote; "And the peace of God, which passeth all understanding, shall keep your hearts and minds through Christ Jesus. (*Philippians 4:7*)."

Remember that the meaning of the word "controversial" is "argument causing." Here is where one of those arguments starts. Without reading what was just written you may find what appears to be a contradiction (That is why it is so important to look at all the scriptures). Jesus is called The Prince of Peace, but in these accounts from Matthew and Luke, He says I am not come to send peace on earth.

MATTHEW 10:34-36 - "Think not that I am come to send peace on earth: I came not to send peace, but a sword. (V.35) For I am come to set a man at variance against his father, and the daughter against her mother, and the daughter in law against her mother in law. (V.36) And a man's foes shall be they of his own household."

<u>**LUKE 12:51-53**</u> - "Suppose ye that I am come to give peace on earth? I tell you, Nay; but rather division: (V.52) For from henceforth there shall be five in one house divided, three against two, and two against three. (V.53) The father shall be divided against the son, and the son against the father; the mother against the daughter, and the daughter against the mother; the mother in law against her daughter in law, and the daughter in law against her mother in law."

Here He is referring to the freedom of free will we are given. Just because one member of a family believes in Jesus, doesn't mean the rest will do so too. This causes division and controversy in the home; all because of Him.

A lot of pictures paint Jesus as a little weak guy in a robe. The robe part is right, but He was anything but weak. As a carpenter of that day it required you to be strong. You worked not only with wood, but rock too. People also view Him as being quiet, helping people and not a trouble maker. Jesus was sinless. However, at times He was controversial as the Prince of Peace. (*Ephesians 4:26: "Be ye angry, and sin not"*)

<u>**JOHN 2:14-17**</u> -"And found in the temple those that sold oxen and sheep and doves, and the

changers of money sitting: (V.15) And when he had made a scourge of small cords, he drove them all out of the temple, and the sheep, and the oxen; and poured out the changers' money, and overthrew the tables; (V.16) And said unto them that sold doves, Take these things hence; make not my Father's house an house of merchandise. (V.17) And His disciples remembered that it was written, The zeal of thine house hath eaten me up (*Psalm 69:9*)."

MATTHEW 23:23-28, 33 -"Woe unto you, scribes and Pharisees, hypocrites! for ye pay tithe of mint and anise and cummin, and have omitted the weightier matters of the law, judgment, mercy, and faith: these ought ye to have done, and not to leave the other undone. (V.24 Ye blind guides, which strain at a gnat, and swallow a camel. (V.25) Woe unto you, scribes and Pharisees, hypocrites! for ye make clean the outside of the cup and of the platter, but within they are full of extortion and excess. (V.26) Thou blind Pharisee, cleanse first that which is within the cup and platter, that the outside of them may be clean also. (V.27) Woe unto you, scribes and Pharisees, hypocrites! for ye are like unto whited sepulchres, which indeed appear beautiful outward, but are within full of dead men's bones, and of all uncleanness. (V.28) Even so ye also outwardly appear righteous unto men, but within ye are full of hypocrisy and iniquity. (V.33) Ye serpents, ye generation of vipers, how can ye escape the damnation of hell?

THE GAME CHANGER

The arrival of Jesus changed everything. He is the dividing line between the Old and the New Testaments. The writer of Hebrews wrote "By so much was Jesus made a surety of a better testament (*Hebrews 7:22*)." The writer also brought up another very interesting point that most people have never thought of. Anyone who knows anything about the Bible should be able to tell you that the first book of the New Testament is Matthew. In publication terms they would be right. However, in scriptural terms they would be wrong. I feel the controversy building! Reading what the author of Hebrews says below hopefully will remove it. Pay close attention to verse seventeen.

HEBREWS 9:14-17 - "How much more shall the blood of Christ, who through the eternal Spirit offered Himself without spot to God, purge your conscience from dead works to serve the living God? (V.15) And for this cause He is the mediator of the New Testament, that by means of death, for the redemption of the transgressions that were under the first testament, they which are called might receive the promise of eternal inheritance. (V.16) <u>For where a testament is, there must also of necessity be the death of the testator</u>. (V.17) For a testament is of force after men are dead: otherwise it is of no strength at all while the testator liveth."

According to this, the book of Acts should be the first book of the New Testament. Matthew, Mark, Luke and John are Scripture (*that's important*), but they are about the historic life *(and death and resurrection)* of Jesus. Acts is where the church of the New Testament is established in the blood of Jesus.

Did I just blow your mind with that thought? That is what Jesus did while He was here on earth. They had the Torah (*our Old Testament*). Jesus told them: "Think not that I am come to destroy the law, or the prophets: I am not come to destroy, but to fulfil (*Matthew 5:17*)," but then He turned around gave them what seemed to be contrary to what they knew.

<u>MATTHEW 5:21&22</u> -"Ye have heard that it was said by them of old time, Thou shalt not kill; and whosoever shall kill shall be in danger of the judgment: (V.22) But I say unto you, That whosoever is angry with his brother without a cause shall be in danger of the judgment: and whosoever shall say to his brother, Raca, shall be in danger of the council: but whosoever shall say, Thou fool, shall be in danger of hell fire.

<u>MATTHEW 5:27&28</u> - "Ye have heard that it was said by them of old time, Thou shalt not commit adultery: (V.28) But I say unto you, That whosoever looketh on a woman to lust after her hath committed adultery with her already in his heart."

MATTHEW 5:38-44 -"Ye have heard that it hath been said, An eye for an eye, and a tooth for a tooth: (V.39) But I say unto you, That ye resist not evil: but whosoever shall smite thee on thy right cheek, turn to him the other also. (V.40) And if any man will sue thee at the law, and take away thy coat, let him have thy cloak also. (V.41) And whosoever shall compel thee to go a mile, go with him twain. (V.42) Give to him that asketh thee, and from him that would borrow of thee turn not thou away. (V.43) Ye have heard that it hath been said, Thou shalt love thy neighbour, and hate thine enemy. (V.44) But I say unto you, Love your enemies, bless them that curse you, do good to them that hate you, and pray for them which despitefully use you, and persecute you."

THE ONLY PERSONTO BE BORN OF A VIRGIN

Are you aware that there are at least a few dozen reported instances of virgin births in history? I thought Jesus was the only person to be born of a virgin, and I still do. His birth and life is the most historically valid. There isn't a single ancient myth that validly declares that someone was born of a virgin, other than the historical account of Jesus Christ. This account is based upon ancient prophecies in the very careful and clear investigation of Luke, a highly respected historian. The fact of the virgin birth of Jesus is distinctive because it's based on ancient prophecy. If you look on the web you will see a list of people whose births are claimed to be virgin born. Some even give parallels to the Messiah of Christianity. Well sorry but they are wrong; this lie was put to rest by1920. In virtually every case the first thing that had happened was some bad scholar had to Christianize the pagan myths to make it seem like it had parallels to Christianity but when you go back to the original myth and De- Christianize the terminologies in the story there is no parallels. The distinguishing characteristic of Jesus' birth is that His has an everlasting kingdom attached to it.

I am not going to waste our time by listing all the reputed instances of virgin births. However I thought a few might be enlightening, if not amusing.

Romulus and Remus were born of a vestal virgin, which was a priestess of the hearth god Vesta sworn to celibacy. His mother claims that the divine impregnated her, yet this is not believed by the King. Romulus and his twin brother, Remus, are tossed in the river and left for dead. (*A "slaughter of the innocents" tale which parallels that of Matthew 2:13-16*). Romulus is hailed as the son of god. He is "snatched away to heaven" by a whirlwind (*It is assumed that the gods took him*), and he makes post mortem appearances. Another story says Rhea Silvia conceived them when their father, the god Mars, visited her in a sacred grove dedicated to him.

A nymph bathing in a river in China is touched by a lotus plant, and the divine Fohi (*also known as Fuxi*) is born.

Krishna or "Chrishna the Saviour" (*note the similarity with Christ*). Now Chrishna was claimed to be born of a chaste virgin called Devaki. His nativity is supposedly heralded by a star. It's said that he was born without a sexual union, by "mental transmission" from the mind of Vasudeva into the womb of Devaki, his mother. However Devaki wasn't a virgin. Before Krishna, Devaki and Vasudeva had seven Sons and Krishna was the eighth one.

Buddha was considered and believed by his followers to have been begotten of God and born of a virgin whose name was Maya. In the life of Buddha we read that he descended on his mother Maya, "in likeness as the heavenly queen, and entered her womb," and was born from her right side, to save the world." It was later reported that Buddha was not said to be born of virgin birth. He is said to have earlier in life, displeased his father, who wanted him to be a warrior and ruler rather than a religious philosopher.

In Greece, the young god Apollo (*who was supposedly born of a virgin*) visits a fair maid (*Perictione*) of Athens, and in 429 B.C. Plato is ushered into the world.

Mithra was a Persian god who was also a virgin birth, but was more than just a tribal god. Mithra was born in a cave and had twelve companions. Mithra's birthday was also on December 25th.

In Siam, a wandering sunbeam caresses a girl in her teens, and the great and wonderful deliverer, Codom, is born.

Virgin births were claimed for many Egyptian Pharaohs, Greek emperors and for Alexander the Great of Greece, and the list goes on. Claimed is the key word here. While these people may have been claimed to be born of a virgin, it doesn't mean they were. These are myths that cannot be authenticated. The birth of Jesus is verified in the Bible. I do believe Luke 1:35 where the angel Gabriel says to Mary: "The Holy Ghost shall come upon thee, and the power of the Highest shall overshadow thee: therefore also that holy thing which shall be born of thee shall be called the Son of God."

HE IS THE ONLY PERSON TO RAISE HIMSELF FROM THE DEAD

Jesus is the only person to rise from dead (*and not die again*). People had been raised from the dead before. Elijah and Elisha had each raised a boy. Jesus raised a widow's son, Jairus's daughter, and Lazarus. However, each one of these died again. Each one also though raised by God, needed someone to aid in their resurrection. In John ten, verses seventeen and eighteen we read that Jesus made this bold statement; "Therefore doth my Father love me, because I lay down my life, that I might take it again. (V.18) No man taketh it from me, but I lay it down of myself. I have power to lay it down, and I have power to take it again. This commandment have I received of my Father." I think it is safe to say, as Jesus did, He laid down His life as God, and as God He raised it up again. No one can make that claim. Let's read Matthews account of what happened proceeding and after Jesus rose from the dead.

MATTHEW 27:62-66 - "Now the next day, that followed the day of the preparation, the chief priests and Pharisees came together unto Pilate, (V.63) Saying, Sir, we remember that that deceiver said, while he was yet alive, After three days I will rise again. (V.64) Command therefore that the sepulchre be made sure until the third day, lest His disciples come by night, and steal him away, and say unto the people, He is risen from the dead: so the last error shall be worse than the first. (V.65)

Pilate said unto them, Ye have a watch: go your way, make it as sure as ye can. (V.66) So they went, and made the sepulchre sure, sealing the stone, and setting a watch."

MATTHEW 28:2-6 - "And, behold, there was a great earthquake: for the angel of the Lord descended from heaven, and came and rolled back the stone from the door, and sat upon it. (V.3) His countenance was like lightning, and his raiment white as snow: (V.4) And for fear of him the keepers did shake, and became as dead men. (V.5) And the angel answered and said unto the women, Fear not ye: for I know that ye seek Jesus, which was crucified. (V.6) He is not here: for He is risen, as He said. Come, see the place where the Lord lay."

MATTHEW 28:11-13 - "Now when they were going, behold, some of the watch came into the city, and showed unto the chief priests all the things that were done. (V.12) And when they were assembled with the elders, and had taken counsel, they gave large money unto the soldiers, (V.13) Saying, Say ye, His disciples came by night, and stole Him away while we slept."

How many people have you heard of that needed their grave watched to make sure someone didn't come and steal the body and say it was resurrected? I've never heard of it.

HE IS THE ONLY WAY TO HEAVEN

One of the popular beliefs of the world today along with "we all serve the same God" is "all roads lead to heaven." I'm here to tell you "Jesus is the only road that leads to heaven." Is that statement controversial, close minded, or truth? According to Jesus (who can't lie), it is truth.

JOHN 14:6 - "Jesus saith unto him, I am the way, the truth, and the life: no man cometh unto the Father, but by me."

Jesus said if you want to get to the Father who is in heaven, you have to go through Him. The Apostle Paul wrote that every knee will bow, and that every tongue should confess that Jesus Christ the way, the truth, and the life.

ROMANS 14:11 - "For it is written, As I live, saith the Lord, every knee shall bow to me, and every tongue shall confess to God (*Isaiah 45:2*)."

PHILIPPIANS 2:9 - "Wherefore God also hath highly exalted Him, and given Him a name which is above every name: (V.10) That at the name of Jesus every knee should bow, of things in heaven, and things in earth, and things under the earth; (V.11) And that every tongue should confess that Jesus Christ is Lord, to the glory of God the

Father."

There are other ways that demonstrated the controversies Jesus caused. I recall a time when He was questioned about why His disciples didn't wash their hands before eating bread, and how He was always breaking tradition. He was defiantly different from what they expected the Messiah to be. That is why they refused to believe who He said He was.

ALL GOD AND ALL MAN

How is it that Jesus can be 100% man and yet be also 100% God? To tell you the truth, I don't know. It's not that I don't believe it could be possible; because nothing is impossible with God. It's just beyond my comprehension. God realized that we as humans would have trouble understanding this. So, He gave us these verses to help us realize there are some things about His ways that we just can't comprehend. You could say He gave us an "out."

ISAIAH 55:8&9 - "For My thoughts are not your thoughts, neither are your ways My ways, saith the LORD. (V.9) For as the heavens are higher than the earth, so are My ways higher than your ways, and My thoughts than your thoughts."

In John 14:8 8 Philip saith to Jesus, "Lord, show us the Father, and it sufficeth us," The word "suffice" means "be enough." In verse nine Jesus saith unto him, "Have I been so long time with you, and yet hast thou not known me, Philip? he that hath seen Me hath seen the Father; and how sayest thou then, Show us the Father?" I'm sure Philip was more baffled than we are about this concept of Jesus being a man and being The Father (*God*). We have the Bible to give us insight into this. We also have the Holy Spirit to lead us into all truths (*John 16:13*).

The following is a list of verses, showing first the frailness of Jesus as a man, and secondly the power of God demonstrated in Him.

<u>AS A MAN</u>

<u>HE BLED</u>:
<u>EPHESIANS 1:7</u> - "In whom we have redemption through His blood, the forgiveness of sins, according to the riches of his grace."

<u>HE GOT HUNGRY AND WAS TEMPTED</u>:
<u>MATTHEW4:2-4</u> - "And when He had fasted forty days and forty nights, He was afterward an hungered (*was hungry*). (V.3) And when <u>the</u>

207

tempter <u>came to Him</u>, he said, If thou be the Son of God, command that these stones be made bread. (V.4) But He answered and said, It is written, Man shall not live by bread alone, but by every word that proceedeth out of the mouth of God."

<u>HEBREWS 2:18</u> - "For in that He himself hath suffered being tempted, He is able to succour them that are tempted."

<u>HE WAS TROUBLED AND WEPT</u>:
<u>JOHN 11:33-36</u> - "When Jesus therefore saw her weeping, and the Jews also weeping which came with her, He groaned in the spirit, and was troubled, (V.34) And said, Where have ye laid him? They said unto him, Lord, come and see. (V.35) Jesus wept. (V.36) Then said the Jews, Behold how He loved him!"

<u>SUFFERED IN AGONY</u>:
<u>LUKE 22:42-44</u> - "Saying, Father, if thou be willing, remove this cup from me: nevertheless not my will, but thine, be done. (V.43) And there appeared an angel unto him from heaven, strengthening Him. (V.44) And being in an agony He prayed more earnestly: and his sweat was as it were great drops of blood falling down to the ground."

<u>HE GOT TIRED AND THIRSTY</u>:
<u>JOHN 4:6&7</u> - "Now Jacob's well was there.

208

Jesus therefore, being wearied with his journey, sat thus on the well: and it was about the sixth hour. (V.7) There cometh a woman of Samaria to draw water: Jesus saith unto her, Give me to drink."

<u>HE SUFFERED REJECTION</u> :
LUKE 22:59-62 -"And about the space of one hour after another confidently affirmed, saying, Of a truth this fellow also was with him: for he is a Galilaean. (V.60) And Peter said, Man, I know not what thou sayest. And immediately, while he yet spake, the cock crew. (V.61) And the Lord turned, and looked upon Peter. And Peter remembered the word of the Lord, how He had said unto him, Before the cock crow, thou shalt deny me thrice. (V.62) And Peter went out, and wept bitterly."

MATTHEW 26:24&25 - "The Son of man goeth as it is written of Him: but woe unto that man by whom the Son of man is betrayed! it had been good for that man if he had not been born. (V.25) Then Judas, which betrayed him, answered and said, Master, is it I? He said unto him, Thou hast said."

LUKE 22:48 - "But Jesus said unto him, Judas, betrayest thou the Son of man with a kiss?"

<u>HE DIED</u>:
LUKE 23:46 - "And when Jesus had cried with a loud voice, He said, Father, into thy hands I

commend my spirit: and having said thus, He gave up the ghost."

PHILIPPIANS 2:8 - "And being found in fashion as a man, He humbled Himself, and became obedient unto death, even the death of the cross."

AS GOD

HE FORGAVE SIN:
MARK 2:5-7 - "When Jesus saw their faith, he said unto the sick of the palsy, Son, thy sins be forgiven thee. (V.6) But there were certain of the scribes sitting there, and reasoning in their hearts, (V. 7) Why doth this man thus speak blasphemies? who can forgive sins but God only?"

LUKE 7:47-49 - "Wherefore I say unto thee, Her sins, which are many, are forgiven; for she loved much: but to whom little is forgiven, the same loveth little. (V.48) And He said unto her, Thy sins are forgiven (V.49) And they that sat at meat with him began to say within themselves, Who is this that forgiveth sins also?"

HE WALKED ON WATER:
MATTHEW 14:25 - "And in the fourth watch of the night Jesus went unto them, walking on the sea."

HE CALMED A STORM:

LUKE 8:23-25 - "But as they sailed He fell asleep: and there came down a storm of wind on the lake; and they were filled with water, and were in jeopardy. (V.24) And they came to Him, and awoke Him, saying, Master, master, we perish. Then He arose, and rebuked the wind and the raging of the water: and they ceased, and there was a calm. (V.25) And He said unto them, Where is your faith? And they being afraid wondered, saying one to another, What manner of man is this! for He commandeth even the winds and water, and they obey him."

HE HAS EVERLASTING LIFE:
JOHN 4:14 - "But whosoever drinketh of the water that I shall give him shall never thirst; but the water that I shall give him shall be in him a well of water springing up into everlasting life."

HE HAS POWER OVER SICKNESS AND DISEASES:
MATTHEW 4:23 - "And Jesus went about all Galilee, teaching in their synagogues, and preaching the gospel of the kingdom, and healing all manner of sickness and all manner of disease among the people."

MATTHEW 10:1 - "And when He had called unto Him His twelve disciples, He gave them power against unclean spirits, to cast them out, and to heal all manner of sickness and all manner of disease."

HE KNOWS ALL THINGS :

JOHN 18:4-6 "Jesus therefore, knowing all things that should come upon Him, (V.5) They answered Him, Jesus of Nazareth. Jesus saith unto them, I am He. And Judas also, which betrayed Him, stood with them (V.6) As soon then as He had said unto them, I am He, they went backward, and fell to the ground."

HE IS ABLE TO SUMMON ANGELS:

MATTHEW 26:52& 53 - "Then said Jesus unto him, Put up again thy sword into his place: for all they that take the sword shall perish with the sword. (V.53) Thinkest thou that I cannot now pray to my Father, and he shall presently give me more than twelve legions of angels?"

HE IS ABLE TO MAKE STONES INTO BREAD:

MATTHEW 4:2-4 - "And when He had fasted forty days and forty nights, He was afterward an hungered (hungry). (V.3) And when the tempter came to him, he said, If thou be the Son of God, command that these stones be made bread. (V.4) But He answered and said, It is written, Man shall not live by bread alone, but by every word that proceedeth out of the mouth of God."

HE IS CHRIST:

<u>**MATTHEW 16:15 -17**</u> - "He saith unto them, But whom say ye that I am? (V.16) And Simon Peter answered and said, Thou art the Christ, the Son of the living God. (V.17) And Jesus answered and said unto him, Blessed art thou, Simon Barjona: for flesh and blood hath not revealed it unto thee, but my Father which is in heaven."

All these things really happened. It was Jesus who did them, Jesus as man, and Jesus as God. Once again, I don't know how this can be. I just have to believe that it is true, and I do.

I'd like us to look at one last point in this chapter. When Isaiah prophesied about the birth of The Messiah, he included some of the names He would be called. It is interesting that "The everlasting Father" is one of those names. These verses leave no question that Jesus was God in the flesh.

<u>**ISAIAH 9:6**</u> - "For unto us a child is born, unto us a son is given: and the government shall be upon His shoulder: and His name shall be called Wonderful, Counsellor, The mighty God, The everlasting Father, The Prince of Peace."

<u>**PHILIPPIANS 2:6-8**</u> - "Who, being in the form of God, thought it not robbery to be equal with God: (V.7) But made himself of no reputation, and took upon him the form of a servant, and was

made in the likeness of men: (V.8) And being found in fashion as a man, He humbled Himself, and became obedient unto death, even the death of the cross."

1 TIMOTHY 3:16 - "And without controversy great is the mystery of godliness: God was manifest in the flesh, justified in the Spirit, seen of angels, preached unto the Gentiles, believed on in the world, received up into glory."

I AM

It may or may not surprise you to learn that when God sent Moses to Egypt, and He told Moses to tell them there that the name of the one who sent him was I AM, wasn't the first time He used that title. Moses isn't mentioned until Exodus, which is the second book of the Bible. Let's look at all the times God used the title of "I am" in the first book, Genesis.

GENESIS 15:1 - "After these things the word of the LORD came unto Abram in a vision, saying, Fear not, Abram: <u>I am thy shield</u>, and thy exceeding great reward"

GENESIS 15:7 - "And He said unto him, <u>I am the LORD that brought thee out</u> of Ur of the Chaldees, to give thee this land to inherit it."

GENESIS 17:1 - "And when Abram was ninety years old and nine, the LORD appeared to Abram, and said unto him, <u>I am the Almighty God</u>; walk before me, and be thou perfect."

GENESIS 26:24 - "And the LORD appeared unto him the same night, and said, <u>I am the God of Abraham</u> thy father: fear not, for <u>I am with thee</u>, and will bless thee, and multiply thy seed for my servant Abraham's sake."

GENESIS 28:13 - "And, behold, the LORD stood above it, and said, <u>I am the LORD God of Abraham</u> thy father, and the God of Isaac: the land whereon thou liest, to thee will I give it, and to thy seed."

GENESIS 28:15 - "And, behold, <u>I am with thee</u>, and will keep thee in all places whither thou goest, and will bring thee again into this land; for I will not leave thee, until I have done that which I have spoken to thee of."

GENESIS 31:13 - "<u>I am the God of Bethel</u>, where thou anointedst the pillar, and where thou vowedst a vow unto me: now arise, get thee out from this land, and return unto the land of thy kindred."

<u>GENESIS 35:11</u> - "And God said unto him, <u>I am God Almighty</u>: be fruitful and multiply; a nation and a company of nations shall be of thee, and kings shall come out of thy loins."

<u>GENESIS 46:3</u> -"And He said, <u>I am God</u>, the God of thy father: fear not to go down into Egypt; for I will there make of thee a great nation."

Then He said to Moses the classic line that many people know so well…

<u>EXODUS 3:14</u> - "And God said unto Moses, <u>I AM THAT I AM</u>: and He said, Thus shalt thou say unto the children of Israel, <u>I AM hath sent me</u> unto you."

You may be saying by now "I thought this was a book about Jesus." Right you are; but we have to remember what John 10:30 says: "I and my Father are one." God spoke those words, but Jesus is the Word, and according to John1:1, we are told that "the Word was God. Jesus used the title of "I Am" many times Himself. On one occasion He was almost stoned for using it. On another it sealed His fate.

<u>JOHN 8:56-58</u> - "Your father Abraham

rejoiced to see my day: and he saw it, and was glad. (V.57) Then said the Jews unto Him, Thou art not yet fifty years old, and hast thou seen Abraham? (V.58) Jesus said unto them, Verily, verily, I say unto you, Before Abraham was, <u>I am</u>.(V.59) Then took they up stones to cast at Him: but Jesus hid Himself, and went out of the temple, going through the midst of them, and so passed by.

<u>**MARK 14:61&62**</u> - "But He held His peace, and answered nothing. Again the high priest asked Him, and said unto Him, Art thou the Christ, the Son of the Blessed? (V.62) And Jesus said, <u>I am</u>: and ye shall see the Son of man sitting on the right hand of power, and coming in the clouds of heaven."

As I mentioned, Jesus used this title many times Himself; here are some of them.

<u>**JOHN 8:23**</u> - "And He said unto them, Ye are from beneath; <u>I am from above</u>: ye are of this world; <u>I am not of this world</u>."

<u>**JOHN 9:5**</u> - "As long as I am in the world, <u>I am the light of the world</u>."

<u>**JOHN 11:25**</u> - "Jesus said unto her, <u>I am the resurrection, and the life</u>: he that believeth in me, though he were dead, yet shall he live."

<u>**JOHN 10:14**</u> - "<u>I am the good shepherd</u>."

217

<u>**JOHN 10:9**</u> - "<u>I am the door</u>."

<u>**JOHN 14:6**</u> - "Jesus saith unto him, <u>I am the way, the truth, and the life</u>: no man cometh unto the Father, but by me."

<u>**JOHN 15:1**</u> - "<u>I am the true vine</u>, and my Father is the husbandman."

<u>**JOHN 15:5**</u> - "<u>I am the vine</u>."

<u>**JOHN 6:48**</u> - "<u>I am that bread of life</u>."

<u>**JOHN 6:51**</u> - "<u>I am the living bread</u>."

<u>**REVELATION 1:8**</u> - "<u>I am Alpha and Omega</u>, the beginning and the ending, saith the Lord, which is, and which was, and which is to come, the Almighty."

The name "I am" signifies; that He is self-existent; He has His being of Himself, and has no dependence upon any other. It is more than any creature, man or angel, can say. Being self-existent, He cannot help but be self-sufficient, and therefore all-sufficient, and the inexhaustible fountain. He is eternal and unchangeable, and always the same, yesterday, to-day, and forever; Malachi 3:6 says: "For I am the LORD, I change not." I want end this chapter with one of my favorite verses that refers to the unchanging God we serve. James 1:17 ends with this phrase, "the Father of lights, with whom is no variableness, neither shadow of turning." You know how it's possible to change your shadow when you change your position to the light that is causing you to cast the shadow. You can appear to be taller or shorter than you actually are. God is the light, and even if He turns, He is always the same.

JESUS ALWAYS WAS AND IS

Contrary to popular belief, the birth of Jesus in Bethlehem was not His beginning. And just in case I didn't mention it, He wasn't born on Christmas day. In the book of Revelation (*1:8*) Jesus Himself said "I am Alpha and Omega, the beginning and the ending, saith the Lord, which is, and which was, and which is to come, the Almighty."

The apostle John (*who wrote the book of Revelation*) wrote this opening statement in his epistle. Then confirmed it again in Revelation 4:8.

JOHN 1:1&2 - "In the beginning was the Word, and the Word was with God, and the Word was God. (V.2) The same was in the beginning

<u>with God</u>."

<u>REVELATION 4:8</u> - "And the four beasts had each of them six wings about him; and they were full of eyes within: and they rest not day and night, saying, Holy, holy, holy, Lord God Almighty, <u>which was, and is, and is to come</u>."

As we can see by these verses, Jesus has been here since the beginning of time. Well then, what about Bethlehem, the angels, the shepherds, and a baby in a manger? That was His physical birth as a human being (*John 1:14 "And the Word was made flesh, and dwelt among us"*).

John also told us in Chapter One verse eighteen that "No man hath seen God at any time." There are two reasons for this. One is found in John 4:24, which tells us that "God is a Spirit," you can't see a spirit. The second reason is what many of the people listed below feared; this is Exodus 33:20: "And He (*God*) said, Thou canst not see my face: for there shall no man see me, and live." So, in The Old Testament Jesus is referred to as "The Angel of the Lord" on several occasions. He appeared as a man to some of the Old Testament saints.

Note: Keep in mind according to Revelation 19:10 "And I fell at his feet to worship him. And he said unto me, See thou do it not: I am thy fellowservant, and of thy brethren that have the testimony of Jesus: worship God. " We are to bow

ONLY to God.

Look back up at John 1:1; it starts with the phrase "In the beginning was the Word, and the Word was with God."We know Jesus is the "Word" John is referring to. He was with God in the beginning. This fact is very evident when reading about the creation of man. Since Jesus was with God in the beginning. Who else could He have been talking to when He said "Let us make man in our image, after our likeness?"

<u>GENESIS 1:26&27</u> - "And God said, Let us make man in our image, after our likeness: and let them have dominion over the fish of the sea, and over the fowl of the air, and over the cattle, and over all the earth, and over every creeping thing that creepeth upon the earth. (V.27) So God created man in His own image, in the image of God created He him; male and female created He them."

Below is a list of people who had an encounter with preincarnate Jesus (*not born in the flesh yet*). The subject of the preincarnate existence of Christ, and His preincarnate works, is important to us for four reasons. First, His preexistence is a necessary attribute. If Christ did not exist prior to His incarnation, then He cannot be God. Second, it is important that the Christian have a firm knowledge of the preincarnate Christ in order to avoid being tossed to and fro by the winds of false doctrine. Third, it gives the Christian a greater appreciation of the unity of the Scriptures. And fourth, it gives the Christian a greater appreciation of certain passages of the Bible.

ABRAHAM:
GENESIS 18:1-3 - "And the LORD appeared unto him in the plains of Mamre: and he sat in the tent door in the heat of the day; (V.2) And he lift up his eyes and looked, and, lo, three men stood by him: and when he saw them, he ran to meet them from the tent door, and bowed himself toward the ground, (V.3) And said, My Lord, if now I have found favour in thy sight, pass not away, I pray thee, from thy servant"

JACOB:
GENESIS 32:24&25, 30 - "And Jacob was left alone; and there wrestled a man with him until the breaking of the day. (V.25) And when he saw that he prevailed not against him, he touched the hollow of his thigh; and the hollow of Jacob's thigh was out of joint, as he wrestled with him. (V.30) And Jacob called the name of the place Peniel: for I have seen God face to face, and my life is preserved."

JOSHUA:
Joshua 5:13 &14 - "And it came to pass, when Joshua was by Jericho, that he lifted up his eyes

and looked, and, behold, there stood a man over against him with his sword drawn in his hand: and Joshua went unto him, and said unto him, Art thou for us, or for our adversaries. (V.14) And he said, Nay; but as captain of the host of the LORD am I now come. And Joshua fell on his face to the earth, and did worship, and said unto him, What saith my Lord unto his servant?"

<u>BALAAM:</u>
<u>NUMBERS 22:31&32</u> - "Then the LORD opened the eyes of Balaam, and he saw the angel of the LORD standing in the way, and his sword drawn in his hand: and he bowed down his head, and fell flat on his face. (V.32) And the angel of the LORD said unto him, Wherefore hast thou smitten thine ass these three times? behold, I went out to withstand thee, because thy way is perverse before me."

<u>GIDEON:</u>
<u>JUDGES 6:11, 22-24</u> - "And there came an angel of the LORD, and sat under an oak. (22) And when Gideon perceived that he was an angel of the LORD, Gideon said, Alas, O Lord GOD! for because I have seen an angel of the LORD face to face. (V.23) And the LORD said unto him, Peace be unto thee; fear not: thou shalt not die. (V.24)Then Gideon built an altar there unto the LORD."

JUDGES 13:20-22 - "For it came to pass, when the flame went up toward heaven from off the altar, that the angel of the LORD ascended in the flame of the altar. And Manoah and his wife looked on it, and fell on their faces to the ground. (V.21) But the angel of the LORD did no more appear to Manoah and to his wife. Then Manoah knew that he was an angel of the LORD. (V.22) And Manoah said unto his wife, We shall surely die, because we have seen God."

ISAIAH:

ISAIAH 6:1 -"In the year that king Uzziah died I saw also the Lord sitting upon a throne, high and lifted up, and his train filled the temple."

I wanted to close this chapter with just a few more of the many verses that state how Jesus has always been since the beginning.

MICAH 5:2 - "But thou, Bethlehem Ephratah, though thou be little among the thousands of Judah, yet out of thee shall he come forth unto Me that is to be ruler in Israel; whose goings forth have been from of old, from everlasting."

LUKE 10:18 - "And He (*Jesus*) said unto them, I beheld Satan as lightning fall from heaven."

JOHN 8:56-58 - "Your father Abraham

rejoiced to see my day: and he saw it, and was glad." (V.57) Then said the Jews unto him, Thou art not yet fifty years old, and hast thou seen Abraham? (V.58) Jesus said unto them, Verily, verily, I say unto you, Before Abraham was, I am."

JOHN 17:24 - "Father, I will that they also, whom thou hast given me, be with me where I am; that they may behold my glory, which thou hast given me: for thou lovedst me before the foundation of the world."

EPHESIANS 1:4 - "According as He hath chosen us in Him before the foundation of the world, that we should be holy and without blame before Him in love."

PHILIPPIANS 2:6-8 - "Who, being in the form of God, thought it not robbery to be equal with God: (V.7) But made Himself of no reputation, and took upon Him the form of a servant, and was made in the likeness of men: (V.8) And being found in fashion as a man, He humbled himself, and became obedient unto death, even the death of the cross."

1 JOHN 1:1&2 - *"That which was from the beginning, which we have heard, which we have seen with our eyes, which we have looked upon, and our hands have handled, of the Word of life; (V.2) (For the life was manifested, and we have seen it, and bear witness, and show unto you that eternal life, which was with the Father, and was manifested unto us;)"*

THE TRINITY

Before we get started in this chapter; I know the word "trinity" is not found in any of the mainstream bibles, but two. These are The Amplified Bible, and The Expanded Bible. It may be interesting to note that in The Amplified Bible the word is only found in its Classic Edition version, and not the Standard Version of this Bible. As you may have guessed from the words "Amplified" and "Expanded." These translations are basically what you will read in any other Bible, but with a little "extra" to bring out the meaning clearer. That is something I do in my books. However, I do this separately, apart from the actual verses. Here are the examples I found compared with the same verse from the King James Version Bible.

<u>The Amplified Bible Classic Edition:</u>
REVELATION 7:10 - "and in a loud voice they cried out, saying, "Salvation [belongs] to our

God who is seated on the throne, and to the Lamb [our salvation is the <u>Trinity</u>'s to give, and to God the Trinity we owe our deliverance]."

<u>REVELATION 7:10</u> -"And cried with a loud voice, saying, Salvation to our God which sitteth upon the throne, and unto the Lamb" - KJV

<u>The Expanded Bible:</u>
<u>ISAIAH 6:8</u> - "Then I heard the Lord's voice, saying, "Whom •can [will] I send [C to speak for God to Israel]? Who will go for us [C referring to God and his heavenly court, or possibly to the <u>Trinity</u>]?" So I said, "Here I am. Send me!"

<u>ISAIAH 6:8</u> - "Also I heard the voice of the Lord, saying, Whom shall I send, and who will go for us? Then said I, Here am I; send me." – KJV

The most difficult thing about the Christian doctrine of the Trinity is that there is no way to perfectly and completely understand it. The Trinity is a concept that is impossible for any human being to fully understand, let alone explain. It would be like this if it was a mathematical equation: $1+1+1=1$. The Bible clearly speaks of: God the Father, God the Son, and God the Holy Spirit; but emphasizes that there is only ONE God; who lives without limitations (*"with God nothing shall be impossible" - Luke 1:37*). He is Spirit (*John 4:24*).

He is infinitely more complex than we are. That is why Jesus the Son can be different from the Father, and yet still the same. The word "Tri" means three, and "Unity" means one, Tri + Unity = Trinity. The dictionary gives the following as its definition:

"God in three forms: In Christianity, God seen in three ways as the Father, the Son Jesus Christ, and the Holy Spirit. 1. A group of three. "

Here are some examples of these three:

MATTHEW 3:16 &17 - "And Jesus, when He was baptized, went up straightway out of the water: and, lo, the heavens were opened unto Him, and he (*John the Baptist*) saw the Spirit of God descending like a dove, and lighting upon Him (*Jesus*): (V.17) And lo a voice from heaven, saying, This is my beloved Son, in whom I am well pleased (Father)."

MATTHEW 28:19 - "Go ye therefore, and teach all nations, baptizing them in the name of the Father, and of the Son, and of the Holy Ghost"

2 CORINTHIANS 13:14 - "The grace of the Lord Jesus Christ, and the love of God, and the communion of the Holy Ghost, be with you all. Amen."

1 JOHN 5:7 - "For there are three that bear record in heaven, the Father, the Word (*Jesus*), and the Holy Ghost: and these three are one."

After reading these verses it cannot be denied that that the Father, the Son, and the Holy Ghost (*Spirit*) are three separate individual beings. Yet,1 John 5:7 tells us "these three are one." As I stated earlier there is no way to perfectly and completely understand the concept of three being three yet one. Don't feel bad if you can't seem to wrap your mind around it. Phillip, who was one of Jesus' disciples, had trouble understanding this very same thing.

JOHN 14:8&9 - "Philip saith unto Him, Lord, show us the Father, and it sufficeth us. (V.9) Jesus saith unto him, Have I been so long time with you, and yet hast thou not known me, Philip? he that hath seen me hath seen the Father; and how sayest thou then, Show us the Father?"

Now granted, Philip was not there when the angel (*probably Gabriel*) came to Joseph as recorded in the scriptures.

MATTHEW 1:20-23 - "But while he thought on these things, behold, the angel of the Lord appeared unto him in a dream, saying, Joseph, thou son of David, fear not to take unto thee Mary thy wife: for that which is conceived in her is of the Holy Ghost. (V.21) And she shall bring forth a son, and thou shalt call his name JESUS: for he shall save his people from their sins. (V.22) Now all this was done, that it might be fulfilled which was spoken of the Lord by the prophet, saying, (V.23) Behold, a virgin shall be with child, and shall bring forth a son, and they shall call his name Emmanuel, which being interpreted is, <u>God with us</u> (*Isaiah 7:14*)."

Other than the verse in Isaiah, Phillip had no idea that Jesus was God in flesh. After all, Jesus had just told him "no man cometh unto the Father, but by me" (*John 14:6*); indicating the two were separate.

He did the same thing in referring to the Holy Ghost. Jesus clearly says "another" will come. Then He tells them they know this one who is coming because "He dwelleth (*lives*) with you." Which indicated this was Him. But then He tells them this one coming "shall be in you," referring to the Holy Ghost.

<u>JOHN 14:16</u> - "And I will pray the Father, and He shall give you another Comforter, that He may abide with you for ever; (V.17) Even the Spirit of truth; whom the world cannot receive, because it seeth Him not, neither knoweth Him: but ye know Him; for He dwelleth with you, and shall be in you."

Before we close this chapter, let's look at a few more verses to hopefully get a little better idea of how this all ties together.

ROMANS 8:26 - "Likewise the Spirit also helpeth our infirmities: for we know not what we should pray for as we ought: but the Spirit itself maketh intercession for us with groanings which cannot be uttered (*We pray to God the Father*)."

ROMANS 8:34 - "Who is he that condemneth? It is Christ that died, yea rather, that is risen again, who is even at the right hand of God, who also maketh intercession for us."

HEBREWS 7:25 - "Wherefore He is able also to save them to the uttermost that come unto God by Him, seeing He ever liveth to make intercession for them."

In closing, the Bible states over and over that there is one God, and that is true. Here are just a few of these verses:

JOHN 10:30 - "I and my Father are one."

MARK 12:32 - "And the scribe said unto Him, Well, Master, thou hast said the truth: for there is one God; and there is none other but He."

ISAIAH 45:5 - "I am the LORD, and there is none else, there is no God beside me."

ISAIAH 45:6 - "That they may know from the rising of the sun, and from the west, that there is none beside me. I am the LORD, and there is none else."

1 CORINTHIANS 8:6 - "But to us there is but one God, the Father, of whom are all things, and we in him; and one Lord Jesus Christ, by whom are all things, and we by Him."

You can't have the Trinity without God, you can't have God without Jesus, and you can't have Jesus without the Holy Spirit.

2 CORINTHIANS 13:14 - "The grace of the Lord <u>Jesus Christ</u>, and the love of <u>God</u>, and the communion of the <u>Holy Ghost</u>, be with you all. Amen."

JESUS AND THE HOLY GHOST

In one sense Jesus and the Holy Spirit are the same. But, in another sense they are not the same. We know that Jesus and the Holy Spirit are both divine since they are members of the Trinity. However, they are not the same person. Each can speak, has a will, recognizes others, etc. This qualifies them as individuals. So, Jesus and the Holy Spirit are not the same (*person*). Yet they are the same in divinity; God the Father, God the Son, and God the Holy Spirit. Allow me to insert a quick note here. The Holy Spirit is always referred to as "He," and never as "it!"

Jesus said that He would send the Holy Spirit in John 15:26: " But when the Comforter is come, whom I will send unto you from the Father, even the Spirit of truth, which proceedeth from the Father, He shall testify of me." So if the Holy Spirit and Jesus were the same, it would not be possible for Jesus to say He would be sending the Holy Spirit. In fact Jesus made it very clear that He must leave, so that the Holy Spirit could come.

JOHN 14:12 - "Verily, verily, I say unto you, He that believeth on me, the works that I do shall he do also; and greater works than these shall he do; because I go unto my Father."

JOHN14:16-18 - "And I will pray the Father, and He shall give you another Comforter, that He may abide with you for ever; (V.17) Even the Spirit of truth; whom the world cannot receive, because it seeth Him not, neither knoweth Him: but ye know Him; for He dwelleth with you, and shall be in you. (V.18) I will not leave you comfortless: I will come to you."

JOHN 14:26 - "But the Comforter, which is the Holy Ghost, whom the Father will send in my name, He shall teach you all things, and bring all things to your remembrance, whatsoever I have said unto you."

<u>JOHN 16:7</u> - "Nevertheless I tell you the truth; It is expedient for you that I go away: for if I go not away, the Comforter will not come unto you; but if I depart, I will send Him unto you."

There are two verses from the scriptures noted above, that have been the subject of much controversy. This has gone as far to say they contradict each other; these are.

<u>JOHN 14:18</u> - "I will not leave you comfortless: I will come to you."

<u>JOHN 16:7</u> - "I will send Him unto you."

In John 14:18 Jesus says "I will come to you," He is referring to Himself. However, in John 16:7 it sounds as if He is sending someone else when He says "I will send Him unto you." Which one of these statements is correct? They both are.

Assuredly, Jesus went back to heaven and sat down at the Fathers right hand. Then, ten days later (*some say nine, depending on where you look*), the Holy Ghost (*Spirit*) filled the disciples in the upper room with the Holy Ghost (Acts 2:1-4). This was a result of what Jesus told them in John 15:26: "But when the Comforter is come, whom I will send unto you from the Father, even the Spirit of truth, which proceedeth from the

Father, He shall testify of me." If this sounds too farfetched to you, remember God was in heaven while He was on earth as Jesus. Why couldn't God be in heaven while being the Holy Spirit on earth? I believe these next two verses show us the dual role of God as Jesus and as the Spirit of God.

ROMANS 8:27 - "And He (*the Holy Spirit*) that searcheth the hearts knoweth what is the mind of the Spirit, because He maketh intercession for the saints according to the will of God."

ROMANS 8:34 - "Who is He that condemneth? It is Christ (*Jesus*) that died, yea rather, that is risen again, who is even at the right hand of God, who also maketh intercession for us."

I hope I didn't throw you off when I used the term "dual role." Jesus is Jesus, and the Holy Spirit is the Holy Spirit. However, we cannot deny that God the Father is also Jesus the Son, and the Holy Spirit. Jesus is not the Holy Spirit, and the Holy Spirit is not Jesus, but both are God (*see more on this subject in The Trinity*). Both have always been, and were not created, but both also proceed from God.

JOHN 8:42 - "Jesus said unto them, If God were your Father, ye would love me: for I proceeded forth and came from God; neither came I of myself, but He sent me."

JOHN 15:26 - "But when the Comforter is come, whom I will send unto you from the Father, even the Spirit of truth, which proceedeth from the Father, he shall testify of me."

Jesus, as I said has always been. He was with the Father in the beginning. However, it wasn't until Mary gave birth (*or became impregnated*), that Jesus proceeded from God; just as with any child that is born would be. The child comes forth from both the man, and the woman. In John 8:42 Jesus tells us "I proceeded forth and from God." Do you see where I'm going with this?

Now, as I said Jesus has always been, so has the Holy Spirit. In Genesis 1:26 God said, "Let us make man in our image, after our likeness." Who do you think He was talking to? Who is the "our" He was referring to? Why it had to be Jesus and the Holy Spirit! Are you aware of the fact that the term "Holy Ghost" is not found in the Old Testament? It is also interesting to note that when the term "holy spirit" is used it is referring to the state of the person's spirit, not the person of the Holy Spirit. Even in Psalm 51:11; where David said "Cast me not away from thy presence; and take not thy holy spirit from me." He was stating that Gods spirit was holy. The Holy Spirit was almost always called "the Spirit of the Lord." He was quite active in the lives of the Old Testament saints. However, He only came "upon" them.

When Jesus went to heaven; God sent the Holy Spirit (Ghost) to be "in" them and us. So, then back to the heart of this paragraph; even though He was always around, Jesus had to return to heaven for the Holy Spirit to proceed from God.

JOHN 7:38& 39 - "He that believeth on Me, as the scripture hath said, out of his belly shall flow rivers of living water. (V.39) (But this spake He of the Spirit, which they that believe on Him should receive: for the Holy Ghost was not yet given; because that Jesus was not yet glorified.)"

We have read that Jesus told His disciples in John 16:7: "Nevertheless I tell you the truth; It is expedient for you that I go away: for if I go not away, the Comforter will not come unto you; but if I depart, I will send Him unto you." Why was it so important to have the Holy Spirit come to them? He went on to tell them in verse thirteen: "Howbeit when He, the Spirit of truth, is come, He will guide you into all truth: for He shall not speak of Himself; but whatsoever He shall hear, that shall He speak: and He will show you things to come." Jesus knew that He had to die to pay the price for the sins of the world. He also knew that He needed to return to heaven that the Spirit can come to His believers. More importantly; He knew His believers would not live forever here on earth. So the Holy Spirit was given to us to carry the word of God forward in a sinful and perverse world until

He returns (*Philippians 2:15*). We are to be witnesses of Him to the glory of God the Father.

JOHN 15:26&27 - "But when the Comforter is come, whom I will send unto you from the Father, even the Spirit of truth, which proceedeth from the Father, He shall testify of me: (V.27) And ye also shall bear witness, because ye have been with me from the beginning."

ACTS 1:8 - "But ye shall receive power, after that the Holy Ghost is come upon you: and ye shall be witnesses unto me both in Jerusalem, and in all Judaea, and in Samaria, and unto the uttermost part of the earth."

I hope you now see that in one sense Jesus and the Holy Spirit are the same. But, in another sense they are not the same.

1 CORINTHIANS 12:3 - "Wherefore I give you to understand, that no man speaking by the Spirit of God calleth Jesus accursed: and that no man can say that Jesus is the Lord, but by the Holy Ghost."

JESUS THE HEALER

MATTHEW 4:24 - *"And His fame went throughout all Syria: and they brought unto Him all sick people that were taken with divers diseases and torments, and those which were possessed with devils, and those which were lunatic, and those that had the palsy; and He healed them."*

There is no denying that Jesus healed many people while He was living here as a human. Some people refer to Him as "The Great Physician." Jesus in a sense denied being a physician in Luke 4:23: "And He said unto them, Ye will surely say unto me this proverb, Physician, heal thyself." However, there was another time He referred to himself in a sense as being a physician in Matthew 9:12: "But when Jesus heard that, He said unto them, They that be whole need not a physician, but they that are sick." Yes, Jesus did a lot of physical healings, but His healings were actually designed to cure people of their unbelief. Jesus told the majority of the people He healed "your faith has made you whole." This was the case for two blind men, and a woman who came to Jesus.

MATTHEW 9:27-30 - "And when Jesus departed thence, two blind men followed Him, crying, and saying, Thou son of David, have mercy on us. (V. 28) And when He was come into the house, the blind men came to Him: and Jesus saith unto them, Believe ye that I am able to do this? They said unto him, Yea, Lord. (V.29) Then touched He their eyes, saying, According to your faith be it unto you. (V.30) And their eyes were opened, spread abroad His fame in all that country.”

MATTHEW 9:20-22 - “And, behold, a woman, which was diseased with an issue of blood twelve years, came behind Him, and touched the hem of His garment: (V.21) For she said within herself, If I may but touch His garment, I shall be whole. (V.22) But Jesus turned Him about, and when He saw her, He said, Daughter, be of good comfort; thy faith hath made thee whole. And the woman was made whole from that hour.”

A note about this woman; Mark and Luke tell us that she had spent all her money on physicians and was not better, but grew worse. Then she finally came to Jesus, believing to be healed. It’s a shame that people will try everything to get well, and then when nothing seems to be working they say “I might as well try God.” What is more of a shame though is when they won’t even “try God” at all. I have nothing against doctors. We are told in Colossians 4:14 that Luke was called “the beloved physician.” I just believe in running to Jesus, before running to the medicine cabinet. King Asa could have used that advice.

<u>**2 CHRONICLES 16:12&13**</u> - "And Asa in the thirty and ninth year of his reign was diseased in his feet, until his disease was exceeding great: yet in his disease he sought not to the LORD, but to the physicians. (V.13) And Asa slept with his fathers, and died"

There were two other cases of faith that need to be mentioned. I don't want you to miss the similarities in these two stories. In each case, it was the faith of someone else that brought about the healing from Jesus. Notice also in each case the fact that the one who got healed was not even present with Jesus when the healing took place. Thirdly, the person making the request was commended by Jesus for their great faith. These are the only two people that received such a statement from Jesus. I find that to be amazing because of the fact that on at least three separate occasions, Jesus said to His own disciples "O ye of little faith." Finally, in each one Jesus is called "Lord."

<u>**MATTHEW 15:22-28**</u> - "And, behold, a woman of Canaan came out of the same coasts, and cried unto Him, saying, Have mercy on me, O Lord, thou son of David; my daughter is grievously vexed with a devil. (V.23) But He answered her not a word. And His disciples came and besought Him, saying, Send her away; for she crieth after us. (V.24) But He answered and said, I

am not sent but unto the lost sheep of the house of Israel (V.25) Then came she and worshipped Him, saying, Lord, help me. (V.26) But He answered and said, It is not meet to take the children's bread, and cast it to dogs. (V.27) And she said, Truth, Lord: yet the dogs eat of the crumbs which fall from their masters' table. (V.28) Then Jesus answered and said unto her, O woman, great is thy faith: be it unto thee even as thou wilt. And her daughter was made whole from that very hour."

MATTHEW 8:5-13 - "And when Jesus was entered into Capernaum, there came unto Him a centurion, beseeching Him, (V.6 And saying, Lord, my servant lieth at home sick of the palsy, grievously tormented. (V.7) And Jesus saith unto him, I will come and heal him. (V.8) The centurion answered and said, Lord, I am not worthy that thou shouldest come under my roof: but speak the word only, and my servant shall be healed. (V.9) For I am a man under authority, having soldiers under me: and I say to this man, Go, and he goeth; and to another, Come, and he cometh; and to my servant, Do this, and he doeth it. (V.10) When Jesus heard it, He marvelled, and said to them that followed, Verily I say unto you, I have not found so great faith, no, not in Israel. (V.11) And I say unto you, That many shall come from the east and west, and shall sit down with Abraham, and Isaac, and Jacob, in the kingdom of heaven. (V.12) But the children of the kingdom shall be cast out into outer darkness: there shall be weeping and gnashing of teeth. (V.13) And Jesus said unto the centurion, Go thy way; and as thou hast believed, so be it done unto thee. And his servant was healed in the selfsame hour."

It is interesting to me to see the different ways Jesus used to healed people who had the same problem. Jesus didn't have a cookie cutter pattern for healing. Just as He deals with us individually. He deals with our sicknesses individually too. We are told in the gospels what some of these afflictions were.

MATTHEW 4:24 - "And His fame went throughout all Syria: and they brought unto Him all sick people that were taken with divers diseases and torments, and those which were possessed with devils, and those which were lunatic, and those that had the palsy; and He healed them."

MATTHEW 15:30 - "And great multitudes came unto Him, having with them those that were lame, blind, dumb, maimed, and many others, and cast them down at Jesus' feet; and He healed them."

LUKE 4:40 - "Now when the sun was setting, all they that had any sick with divers diseases brought them unto Him; and He laid his hands on every one of them, and healed them."

LUKE 6:17-19 - "And He came down with them, and stood in the plain, and the company of His disciples, and a great multitude of people out of all Judaea and Jerusalem, and from the sea coast of Tyre and Sidon, which came to hear Him, and to be healed of their diseases; (V.18) And they that were vexed with unclean spirits: and they were healed. (V.19) And the whole multitude sought to touch Him: for there went virtue out of Him, and healed them all."

"He healed them all." Indeed He did, no matter what the situation was. What I want us to do now is look at how He healed those that were afflicted with the same ailment.

BLIND:
MATTHEW 9:27-30 - "And when Jesus departed thence, two blind men followed Him, crying, and saying, Thou son of David, have mercy on us. (V. 28) And when He was come into the house, the blind men came to Him: and Jesus saith unto them, Believe ye that I am able to do this? They said unto him, Yea, Lord. (V. 29) Then touched He their eyes, saying, According to your faith be it unto you. (V. 30) And their eyes were opened, spread abroad His fame in all that country."

MARK 8:23-25 - "And He took the blind man by the hand, and led him out of the town; and when He had spit on his eyes, and put His hands upon him, He asked him if he saw ought. (V. 24) And he looked up, and said, I see men as trees, walking. (V. 25) After that He put His hands again upon his eyes, and made him look up: and he was restored, and saw every man clearly."

<u>MARK 10:51&52</u> - "And Jesus answered and said unto him, What wilt thou that I should do unto thee? The blind man said unto Him, Lord, that I might receive my sight. (V. 52) And Jesus said unto him, Go thy way; thy faith hath made thee whole. And immediately he received his sight, and followed Jesus in the way."

<u>LUKE 18:41-43</u> - "Saying, What wilt thou that I shall do unto thee? And he said, Lord, that I may receive my sight. (V. 42) And Jesus said unto him, Receive thy sight: thy faith hath saved thee. (V.43) And immediately he received his sight, and followed Him, glorifying God: and all the people, when they saw it, gave praise unto God."

<u>JOHN 9:6&7</u> - "When He had thus spoken, He spat on the ground, and made clay of the spittle, and He anointed the eyes of the blind man with the clay, (V. 7) And said unto him, Go, wash in the pool of Siloam, (which is by interpretation, Sent.) He went his way therefore, and washed, and came seeing."

<u>LEPROSY</u>:

<u>MATTHEW 8:3</u> - "And Jesus put forth his hand, and touched him, saying, I will; be thou clean. And immediately his leprosy was cleansed."

<u>LUKE 17:12&14</u> - "And as He entered into a certain village, there met him ten men that were lepers, (V.14) And when He saw them, He said unto them, Go show yourselves unto the priests. And it came to pass, that, as they went, they were cleansed."

<u>DEAFNESS</u>:

<u>MARK 7:32-35</u> - "And they bring unto Him one that was deaf, and had an impediment in his speech; and they beseech Him to put his hand upon him. (V. 33) And He took him aside from the multitude, and put His fingers into his ears, and He spit, and touched his tongue; (V.34) And looking up to heaven, He sighed, and saith unto him, Ephphatha, that is, Be opened. (V.35) And straightway his ears were opened, and the string of his tongue was loosed, and he spake plain."

<u>MARK 9:25</u> - "When Jesus saw that the people came running together, He rebuked the foul spirit, saying unto him, Thou dumb and deaf spirit, I charge thee, come out of him, and enter no more into him."

<u>LAME</u>:

MATTHEW 21:14 - "And the blind and the lame came to Him in the temple; and He healed them."

JOHN 5:5-9 - "And a certain man was there, which had an infirmity thirty and eight years. (V.6) When Jesus saw him lie, and knew that he had been now a long time in that case, He saith unto him, Wilt thou be made whole? (V.7) The impotent man answered him, Sir, I have no man, when the water is troubled, to put me into the pool: but while I am coming, another steppeth down before me. (V.8) Jesus saith unto him, Rise, take up thy bed, and walk. (V.9) And immediately the man was made whole, and took up his bed, and walked: and on the same day was the sabbath."

RAISING DEAD:
LUKE 7:14&15 - (*Widows son*) "And He came and touched the bier: and they that bare him stood still. And He said, Young man, I say unto thee, Arise. (V. 15) And he that was dead sat up"

LUKE 8:53&55 - (*Jairus's daughter*) "knowing that she was dead. (V.54) And He put them all out, and took her by the hand, and called, saying, Maid, arise. (V. 55) And her spirit came again, and she arose straightway"

JOHN 11:43&44 - (*Lazarus*) "And when He thus had spoken, He cried with a loud voice,

Lazarus, come forth. (V.44) And he that was dead came forth"

<u>PALSY</u>:
<u>MATTHEW 8:5-13</u> - "And when Jesus was entered into Capernaum, there came unto him a centurion, beseeching him, (V.6) And saying, Lord, my servant lieth at home sick of the palsy, grievously tormented. (V.7) And Jesus saith unto him, I will come and heal him. (V.8) The centurion answered and said, Lord, I am not worthy that thou shouldest come under my roof: but speak the word only, and my servant shall be healed. (V.9) For I am a man under authority, having soldiers under me: and I say to this man, Go, and he goeth; and to another, Come, and he cometh; and to my servant, Do this, and he doeth it. (V.10) When Jesus heard it, he marvelled, and said to them that followed, Verily I say unto you, I have not found so great faith, no, not in Israel. (V.11) And I say unto you, That many shall come from the east and west, and shall sit down with Abraham, and Isaac, and Jacob, in the kingdom of heaven. (V.12) But the children of the kingdom shall be cast out into outer darkness: there shall be weeping and gnashing of teeth. (V.13) And Jesus said unto the centurion, Go thy way; and as thou hast believed, so be it done unto thee. And his servant was healed in the selfsame hour."

<u>MATTHEW 9:2,6&7</u>- "And, behold, they

brought to Him a man sick of the palsy, lying on a bed: and Jesus seeing their faith said unto the sick of the palsy; Son, be of good cheer; thy sins be forgiven thee. (V.6) But that ye may know that the Son of man hath power on earth to forgive sins, (then saith He to the sick of the palsy,) Arise, take up thy bed, and go unto thine house. (V.7) And he arose, and departed to his house.

<u>OTHER</u>:
<u>MATTHEW 12:10-13</u> - "And, behold, there was a man which had his hand withered. And they asked him, saying, Is it lawful to heal on the sabbath days? (V.12) Wherefore it is lawful to do well on the sabbath days. (V.13) Then saith He to the man, Stretch forth thine hand. And he stretched it forth; and it was restored whole, like as the other."

<u>MARK 6:5&6</u> - "And He could there do no mighty work, save that He laid His hands upon a few sick folk, and healed them.(V.6) And He marvelled because of their unbelief (*lack of faith*)."

We've read above how those multitudes of people were brought to Jesus in various ways, and He healed them all. However, it doesn't take a brain surgeon to realize that He didn't heal every person who was sick. Most everyone Jesus healed was brought to Him, or sought Him out, with a few exceptions. One of those times is found in the fifth chapter of John. It was the man at the pool of Bethesda who had an infirmity for thirty eight years. Jesus walked up to him and asked him "Wilt thou be made whole?" The man answered back "I have no man, when the water is troubled, to put me into the pool." If you ask me, this was an unintentional insult to Jesus. He's ready to heal this man, and the man thinks it will come through the water. Jesus must have had compassion on him, and said to him, "Rise, take up thy bed, and walk;" and immediately the man was made whole. I know we read this not too far back, but this is not a review. What I want us to look at are the verses that lead up to this man's healing.

JOHN 5:1-4 - "After this there was a feast of the Jews; and Jesus went up to Jerusalem. (V.2) Now there is at Jerusalem by the sheep market a pool, which is called in the Hebrew tongue Bethesda, having five porches. (V.3) In these lay a great multitude of impotent folk, of blind, halt, withered, waiting for the moving of the water. (V.4) For an angel went down at a certain season into the pool, and troubled the water: whosoever then first after the troubling of the water stepped in was made whole of whatsoever disease he had."

Verse three tells us there was a great multitude of impotent (*weak*) folk, who were blind, halt, and withered. Jesus must have walked through these people, but only healed that one man. Maybe it was because He knew after the man had been lying there for so long. He would never be able to get into the water when it was troubled. I really don't know why. After all, the man never called out to Jesus, he wasn't brought to Him either. Nobody came to Jesus and requested a healing for him. He didn't even know it was Jesus that had healed him; and to top it off, this infirmity was a result of his sin.

<u>JOHN 5:14</u> - "Afterward Jesus findeth him in the temple, and said unto him, Behold, thou art made whole: sin no more, lest a worse thing come unto thee."

Why didn't Jesus heal the other people at the pool? I say once again "I don't know." There is something I do know though. God is wiser than we are. His ways are always right. He is God Almighty, who are we to question His actions. God does nothing by chance or haphazardly. God has purpose in all He does. This also means that God also has a time for everything He does, as well.

We know for a fact that Jesus did not heal the lame man at the temple gate called Beautiful during His human lifetime. In Acts three we are told he was "laid daily at the gate." There is no doubt that he was there when Jesus went in and out of the temple, yet Jesus never healed him; then. The man was later healed by "the name of Jesus" in verse six.

Another thing we should consider is there was already a means of healing in place (*the pool*), but we just don't know. The Scripture doesn't say anything about Jesus healing anyone else at that time. Maybe He healed others. Maybe He didn't.

Jesus caught a lot of flak for healing this man, and telling him to take up his bed, and walk on the Sabbath day.

JOHN 5:16 "And therefore did the Jews persecute Jesus, and sought to slay him, because He had done these things on the sabbath day."

Just think what might have happened if He went in there and healed all the ones who were lying at the pool. The people would have had a fit!

If you're still having a hard time understanding how God would heal some but not others. I've included these two sections of Scripture.

LUKE 4:24-27 - "And He said, Verily, I say unto you, No prophet is accepted in his own country. (V. 25) But I tell you of a truth, many widows were in Israel in the days of Elias (Elijah), when the heaven was shut up three years and six months, when great famine was throughout all the land; (V. 26) But unto none of them was Elias sent, save unto Sarepta, a city of Sidon, unto a woman that was a widow. (V. 27) And many lepers were in Israel in the time of Eliseus (Elisha) the prophet;

and none of them was cleansed, saving Naaman the Syrian."

ROMANS 9:15-18 - "For He saith to Moses, I will have mercy on whom I will have mercy, and I will have compassion on whom I will have compassion (*Exodus 33:19*). (V. 16) So then it is not of him that willeth, nor of him that runneth, but of God that showeth mercy. (V.17) For the scripture saith unto Pharaoh, Even for this same purpose have I raised thee up, that I might show my power in thee, and that my name might be declared throughout all the earth. (V.18) Therefore hath He mercy on whom He will have mercy, and whom He will He hardeneth."

There are many other aspects of the healings Jesus preformed. Remember, this is just a chapter not a whole book about the subject. I'll close with what Jesus told the two disciples of John, when they came and asked Him "Art thou He that should come, or do we look for another? (*Matthew 11:3*)"

MATTHEW 11:4-5 - "Jesus answered and said unto them, Go and show John again those things which ye do hear and see: (V. 5) The blind receive their sight, and the lame walk, the lepers are cleansed, and the deaf hear, the dead are raised up, and the poor have the gospel preached to them."

THEY TRIED TO KILL HIM

__LUKE 23:46__ -"And when Jesus had cried with a loud voice, he said, Father, into thy hands I commend my spirit: and having said thus, He gave up the ghost."

Most everyone reading this book by now should know that Jesus died; really died. Some people say He only appeared to be dead, and really didn't die at all. I don't see how you can get around John 19:34: "But one of the soldiers with a spear pierced his side, and forthwith came there out blood and water." Of course His story didn't end there. He was buried, and rose from the dead on the third day. Just as He told his disciples before it happened.

__MATTHEW 16:21__ - "From that time forth began Jesus to show unto his disciples, how that he must go unto Jerusalem, and suffer many things of the elders and chief priests and scribes, and be killed, and be raised again the third day."

Yes, He finally died; it was His time (*Matthew 26:18 - "My time is at hand"*). I say finally, because His life was threatened many times before He actually did die. Even before He was born His life was in danger. Below are two examples of this. One was a prophet vision given to John about a dragon who was ready to devour Him as soon as

He was born (*when you read verse 5, there is no denying it's referring to Jesus*). The second is the more familiar story of the wise men bringing their gifts to Jesus. In reading this story, you can't help but wonder if the dragon mentioned in Revelation was pointing to Herod. The dragon wanted to devour the child; while Herod sought to destroy him.

REVELATION 12:3-5 - "And there appeared another wonder in heaven; and behold a great red dragon, having seven heads and ten horns, and seven crowns upon his heads. (V.4) And his tail drew the third part of the stars of heaven, and did cast them to the earth: and <u>the dragon stood before the woman which was ready to be delivered, for to devour her child as soon as it was born</u>. (V.5) And she brought forth a man child, who was to rule all nations with a rod of iron: and her child was caught up unto God, and to his throne."

MATTHEW 2:8,12,13.16 - "And he sent them to Bethlehem, and said, Go and search diligently for the young child; and when ye have found Him, bring me word again, that I may come and worship him also. (V.12) And being warned of God in a dream that they should not return to Herod, they departed into their own country another way. (V.13) And when they were departed, behold, the angel of the Lord appeareth to Joseph in a dream, saying, Arise, and take the young child and His mother, and flee into Egypt, and be thou there until I bring thee word: for Herod will seek the young child to destroy him. (V.16) Then Herod, when he saw that he was mocked of the wise men, was exceeding wroth, and sent forth, and <u>slew all the children that were in Bethlehem, and in all the coasts thereof, from two years old and under</u>, according to the time which he had diligently inquired of the wise men."

Those verses were from the time when He was just a child. What about when He grew up and was ministering to the needs of the people; or "doing good" as Luke put it in Acts 10:38. Surely no one would want to kill Him then. I wish I could say of course not, but it wouldn't be the truth.

<u>MATTHEW 26:3</u> - "Then assembled together the chief priests, and the scribes, and the elders of the people, unto the palace of the high priest, who was called Caiaphas, (V.4) And consulted that they might take Jesus by subtlety, and kill Him."

<u>LUKE 13:31</u>- "The same day there came certain of the Pharisees, saying unto him, Get thee out, and depart hence: for Herod will kill thee."

<u>LUKE 22:2</u> - "And the chief priests and scribes sought how they might kill him; for they feared the people."

JOHN 7:1 - "After these things Jesus walked in Galilee: for he would not walk in Jewry, because the Jews sought to kill him."

JOHN 7:19&20 - "Did not Moses give you the law, and yet none of you keepeth the law? Why go ye about to kill me? (V.20) The people answered and said, Thou hast a devil: who goeth about to kill thee?"

JOHN 11:7&8 - "Then after that saith he to his disciples, Let us go into Judaea again. (V.8) His disciples say unto him, Master, the Jews of late sought to stone thee; and goest thou thither again?"

If Jesus was going about doing good; why did the people want to kill Him? The
best answer is that the people didn't understand Him. His own disciples didn't even understand Him fully. Let's first look at the leaders of the day. The priests, Pharisees, scribes, and elders were all jealous of Him.

JOHN 11:45-53 - "Then many of the Jews which came to Mary, and had seen the things which Jesus did, believed on Him. (V.46) But some of them went their ways to the Pharisees, and told them what things Jesus had done. (V.47) Then gathered the chief priests and the Pharisees a council, and said, What do we? for this man doeth many miracles. (V.48) If we let him thus alone, all men will believe on him: and the Romans shall come and take away both our place and nation. (V.49) And one of them, named Caiaphas, being the high priest that same year, said unto them, Ye know nothing at all, (V.50) Nor consider that it is expedient for us, that one man should die for the people, and that the whole nation perish not. (V.51) And this spake he not of himself: but being high priest that year, he prophesied that Jesus should die for that nation; (V.52) And not for that nation only, but that also he should gather together in one the children of God that were scattered abroad. (V.53) Then from that day forth they took counsel together for to put him to death."

Secondly, the Jewish people did not understand Him. As I said elsewhere in this book; Jesus was controversial. He said and did things the people never heard or saw before. He broke the Sabbath laws, and then explained that what He did was okay. He said things like "you have heard it said" and tell them of a law they were to follow. Then say "but I tell you..." and finish with His twist on hat law. There was one time He lost followers because of what He had said.

JOHN 6:53,60,66 - "Then Jesus said unto them, Verily, verily, I say unto you, Except ye eat the flesh of the Son of man, and drink his blood, ye have no life in you." V.60 Many therefore of his disciples, when they had heard this, said, This is an hard saying; who can hear it? (V.66) From that time many of his disciples went back, and walked no more with him."

The scripture says that these people walked away and walked with Him no more. Other people were not as nice to Him. Here are at least two occasions where they wanted to stone Him because of something He said.

JOHN 8:56-59 - "Your father Abraham rejoiced to see my day: and he saw it, and was glad. (V.57) Then said the Jews unto him, Thou art not yet fifty years old, and hast thou seen Abraham? (V.58) Jesus said unto them, Verily, verily, I say unto you, Before Abraham was, I am. (V.59) Then took they up stones to cast at him: but Jesus hid himself, and went out of the temple, going through the midst of them, and so passed by."

JOHN 10:28-33 - "And I give unto them eternal life; and they shall never perish, neither shall any man pluck them out of my hand. (V.29) My Father, which gave them me, is greater than all; and no man is able to pluck them out of my Father's hand. (V.30) I and my Father are one. (V.31) Then the Jews took up stones again to stone him. (V.32) Jesus answered them, Many good works have I showed you from my Father; for which of those works do ye stone me? (V.33) The

Jews answered him, saying, For a good work we stone thee not; but for blasphemy; and because that thou, being a man, makest thyself God.”

As can see Jesus was no stranger to being threatened with death. He knew it would happen. However, He had a plan and a purpose to complete the task His Father sent Him to do, and wasn't going to die until “it is finished.”

<u>JESUS AND ALCOHOL</u>

Whenever the subject of drinking alcohol and what the Bible has to say about it you will get one of three answers. “Well Jesus drank wine”, “Jesus turned water into wine,” or “it's wrong.” Yes, Jesus did drink wine. We are told that Jesus drank wine (*Luke 7:34*) and we know that He did not sin; therefore, it is not wrong or bad if we do the same as our Savior. In fact, Jesus' own mother, Mary, asked her son to make more of it at the marriage feast in Cana. I feel like I would be neglecting a crucial point about the story of the wedding feast if I didn't mention that Jesus turned water into wine only on this one occasion, and the miracle was never duplicated by his disciples or anyone else.

Jesus did not preach against the use of wine; instead He did like most other people of His day. He drank wine in moderation. In ancient times it was normally diluted with water for drinking and was one of the principal beverages at that time, as it still is today (*just look how large the wine section is at a grocery store*). In New Testament times, the water was not very clean. Without modern sanitation, the water was often filled with bacteria, viruses, and all kinds of contaminants. The same is still true in many third-world countries today. As a result, people often drank wine or grape juice because it was far less likely to be contaminated. In 1 Timothy 5:23, Paul was instructing Timothy to stop drinking water only (*which was probably causing his stomach problems*) and instead drink wine. In that day, wine was fermented (*containing alcohol*), but not necessarily to the degree it is today.

Throughout the New Testament, the Greek word translated to "wine" is oinos. Which was the common Greek word for wine; wine that was fermented or alcoholic. This was the word used for the wine Jesus had created at the wedding feast, and for the wine they had run out of. This the same Greek word for the wine Jesus created and is also the same word that is used in Ephesians 5:18, "...be not drunk with wine..." Obviously, getting drunk from drinking wine requires the presence of alcohol.

Yes, Jesus also changed water into wine. So,

let's look at this issue of Jesus turning water into wine. While everyone is quick to say that Jesus turned water into wine. For some reason, it was only John who felt the need to mention this account. Verse two tells us His disciples were there. However, the account does not appear in any other place in the Bible but chapter two in the book of John.

<u>JOHN 2:1-11</u>- "And the third day there was a marriage in Cana of Galilee; and the mother of Jesus was there: (V.2) And both Jesus was called, and His disciples, to the marriage.(V.3) And when they wanted wine, the mother of Jesus saith unto Him, They have no wine.(V.4) Jesus saith unto her, Woman, what have I to do with thee? mine hour is not yet come.(V.5) His mother saith unto the servants, Whatsoever He saith unto you, do it.(V.6) And there were set there six waterpots of stone, after the manner of the purifying of the Jews, containing two or three firkins apiece.(V.7) Jesus saith unto them, Fill the waterpots with water. And they filled them up to the brim. (V.8) And He saith unto them, Draw out now, and bear unto the governor of the feast. And they bare it. (V.9) When the ruler of the feast had tasted the water that was made wine, and knew not whence it was: (but the servants which drew the water knew;) the governor of the feast called the bridegroom, (V.10) And saith unto him, Every man at the beginning doth set forth good wine; and when men have well drunk, then that which is worse: but thou hast kept the good wine until now. (V.11) This beginning of miracles did Jesus in Cana of Galilee, and manifested forth His glory; and His disciples believed on Him."

You will note that I added the eleventh verse into the text. That's because verse eleven is actually the most important verse of this whole story. It's not that Jesus turned water into wine. It's that Jesus could turn water into wine. It was the first miracle He did; and because of this it "manifested forth His glory; and His disciples believed on Him."

There is an argument that by creating alcoholic wine, Jesus would have been promoting drunkenness, which the Bible clearly identifies as sinful. This is not a valid argument. Was Jesus promoting gluttony when He multiplied the fishes and loaves far beyond what the people needed? Of course it doesn't; creating a substance that can be abused not make one responsible when another person foolishly chooses to abuse it. Jesus creating alcoholic wine was in no sense encouraging drunkenness.

Have you ever wondered if the wine at the Last Supper was fermented?

If you attend churches of the Christian faith, you will find one thing they all have in common; the sacrament of The Lord's Supper. There are as many differences in the way it is celebrated as there are denominations. Some turn down the lights, while others leave them on. Some play music and others don't. Some take it as a group, while others partake individually. Some use wine, while others use grape juice. However, there are two things that are always constant; the bread and the cup.   The reason this is called "The Lord's Supper," is because Jesus instituted it. They had many meals with bread and wine before this, but not with the same meaning as this one had. In actuality, they were going to celebrate The Feast of Unleavened Bread, which is called the Passover.

MATTHEW 26:17 - "Now the first day of the feast of unleavened bread the disciples came to Jesus, saying unto Him, Where wilt thou that we prepare for thee to eat the Passover?"

LUKE 22:15- "And He said unto them, With desire I have desired to eat this Passover with you before I suffer"

This supper was going to be the last time Jesus sat and ate with His disciples while He was still in His human body. He washed their feet, told of His betrayal, told Peter he would deny Him three times (*Luke 22:34*), and gave new meaning to the bread and the cup (*wine*).

MATTHEW 26:26-28- "And as they were

eating, Jesus took bread, and blessed it, and brake it, and gave it to the disciples, and said, Take, eat; this is my body. (V.27) And He took the cup, and gave thanks, and gave it to them, saying, Drink ye all of it; (V.28) For this is my blood of the new testament, which is shed for many for the remission of sins." (*Luke 22:19 adds "this do in remembrance of me."*)

<u>Paul gave this account in First Corinthians:</u>
<u>1 CORINTHIANS 11:23-26</u>- "For I have received of the Lord that which also I delivered unto you, That the Lord Jesus the same night in which He was betrayed took bread: (V.24) And when He had given thanks, he brake it, and said, Take, eat: this is my body, which is broken for you: this do in remembrance of me. (V.25) After the same manner also He took the cup, when he had supped, saying, This cup is the new testament in my blood: this do ye, as oft as ye drink it, in remembrance of me. (V.26) For as often as ye eat this bread, and drink this cup, ye do show the Lord's death till he come."

That was history and I hope you knew it. So let's see why this story s important to us; besides the obvious. In every account of The Lord's Supper, the wine is referred to as "the cup." So, how do you know there was wine I the cup? Because Jesus told us so!

MATTHEW 26:29 - "But I say unto you, I will not drink henceforth of this fruit of the vine, until that day when I drink it new with you in my Father's kingdom."

LUKE 22:17 & 18- "And He took the cup, and gave thanks, and said, Take this, and divide it among yourselves: (V.18) For I say unto you, I will not drink of the fruit of the vine, until the kingdom of God shall come." (*See Acts 10:41*)

The term "fruit of the vine" always means wine. Now, Jesus drank wine on other occasions. Here, He chose not to. He ate of the bread (*Matthew 26:23 -"He that dippeth his hand with me in the dish, the same shall betray me."*), but He didn't drink the wine. I have a feeling that because of its symbolic meaning (*Matthew 26:28 - "for the remission of sins"*), Jesus, who was sinless, didn't need to have His sin remitted (*forgiven*).

Some who question whether this cup was alcoholic wine, will say "there was no indication of its fermentation." This brings me to my next point. After they eaten; Jesus took them out into The Mount of Olives. They came to a place in which was a garden called Gethsemane, and saith unto the disciples, "Sit ye here, while I go and pray yonder." Matthew 26:38 says that He told them, "My soul is exceeding sorrowful, even unto death: tarry ye here, and watch with me." Then He prayed.

MATTHEW 26:39- " And He went a little farther, and fell on His face, and prayed, saying, O my Father, if it be possible, let this cup pass from me: nevertheless not as I will, but as thou wilt."

To make my point I need to insert the account of the events that took place after Jesus had gone to pray. Remember He had told them to "watch with Him."

MATTHEW 26:40-45- "And He cometh unto the disciples, and findeth them asleep, and saith unto Peter, What, could ye not watch with me one hour? (V.41) Watch and pray, that ye enter not into temptation: the spirit indeed is willing, but the flesh is weak. (V.42) He went away again the second time, and prayed, saying, O my Father, if this cup may not pass away from me, except I drink it, thy will be done. (V.43) And He came and found them asleep again: for their eyes were heavy. (V.44) And He left them, and went away again, and prayed the third time, saying the same words. (V.45) Then cometh He to His disciples, and saith unto them, Sleep on now, and take your rest: behold, the hour is at hand, and the Son of man is betrayed into the hands of sinners."

Let me explain why I thought this section of Scripture was so important to my point. Now, I might be "reaching" but hear me out. Jesus was the only one who didn't drink of "the cup." There is no telling how much the disciples had drunk. I realize Jesus was going through a horrible ordeal, knowing what was about to happen. I can understand why He was sleepless. However, His disciples who were charged to watch with Him couldn't stay awake. If there was no indication of the cups ingredients being fermented, don't you think at least one of the disciples could have stayed awake?

Above, I said that I was reaching, but I don't think I am reaching too far. Remember, Jesus instituted The Lord's Supper, and the items that went with it (the bread and the wine). So, when celebrating the sacrament, wouldn't they have included what He had included? Of course they would. When something has the spiritual implications as this you want to do it right.1 CORINTHIANS 11:26 tells us "For as often as ye eat this bread, and drink this cup, ye do show the Lord's death till he come." With this in mind, Jesus must have used fermented wine in the cup; or the letter Paul was writing to the Corinthians would be useless.

1 CORINTHIANS 11:20&21- "When ye come together therefore into one place, this is not to eat the Lord's Supper. (V.21) For in eating every one taketh before other his own supper: and one is hungry, and another is drunken."

With that said, it seems clear that Jesus served His disciples wine at the original Lord's Supper, which took place at the last supper. The gospels portray the Last Supper as a Passover meal. Wine was the drink used in the Passover feast. When Jesus picked up the Passover cup, it was a cup of wine. The unleavened bread was also a part of the Passover feast, and was used by Jesus in the institution of the Lord's Supper. After the first communion Jesus said, "I will not drink of the fruit of the vine, until the kingdom of God shall come" (Luke 22:18), indicating that wine was the drink he had just used in the institution of it. It seems suitable to use the same elements in the Lord's Supper that Jesus used in the origination of it.

If Jesus had been using grape juice to fill the cup, and if the Corinthians were doing everything Jesus instituted in the Lord's Supper; how did some end up drunk? The problem here was with some of the people were coming to the temple early. They would eat up all the bread, and drink up all the wine used for the Lord's Supper. Then when the others came everything was gone so that they couldn't even have the Lord's Supper. As mentioned above, some of the people drank so much of the wine used for the Lord's Supper that they were getting drunk. You can't get drunk on grape juice! The question of whether it is acceptable to serve either wine or grape juice during communion is a debate that can be very divisive. People defend their position with great zeal; and in an effort to defend the position they've taken, many people seem to lose sight of the greater issue, and that is what the liquid in the cup represents, the shed blood of our Lord and Savior establishing the New Covenant. I hope this has answered some of your questions.

<u>TEMPTED</u>

It's hard to believe that the Devil tempted Jesus. Notice that I didn't say he tried to tempt Jesus. He did tempt Him. Jesus just didn't give into the temptation. What were the reasons for the temptations? Satan's aim in all the temptations, was, to get Jesus to sin against God, and so to render Him forever incapable of being a sacrifice for the sins of others.

<u>**HEBREWS 4:15**</u> - " For we have not an high priest which cannot be touched with the feeling of our infirmities; but was <u>in all points tempted</u> like as we are, yet without sin."

Let's look at Matthews's account of "The

Temptation of Jesus Christ."

MATTHEW 4:1-11 - "Then was Jesus led up of the Spirit into the wilderness to be tempted of the devil. (V.2) And when He had fasted forty days and forty nights, He was afterward an hungered. (V.3) And when the tempter came to Him, he said, If thou be the Son of God, command that these stones be made bread. (V.4) But He answered and said, It is written, Man shall not live by bread alone, but by every word that proceedeth out of the mouth of God. (V.5) Then the devil taketh Him up into the holy city, and setteth him on a pinnacle of the temple, (V.6) And saith unto Him, If thou be the Son of God, cast thyself down: for it is written, He shall give his angels charge concerning thee: and in their hands they shall bear thee up, lest at any time thou dash thy foot against a stone. (V.7) Jesus said unto him, It is written again, Thou shalt not tempt the Lord thy God. (V.8) Again, the devil taketh Him up into an exceeding high mountain, and showeth Him all the kingdoms of the world, and the glory of them; (V.9) And saith unto Him, All these things will I give thee, if thou wilt fall down and worship me. (V.10) Then saith Jesus unto him, Get thee hence, Satan: for it is written, Thou shalt worship the Lord thy God, and Him only shalt thou serve. (V.11) Then the devil leaveth Him, and, behold, angels came and ministered unto him."

You may be thinking that it was easy for Jesus

to resist temptation. Let me assure you temptation is not easy for anyone. That's why it's called temptation! Satan will not tempt you with something you don't desire. Remember the writer of Hebrews 4:15 told us: He (*Jesus*) "was in all points tempted like as we are." He was tired and hungry. He could have made the stones bread. Satan said "If thou be the Son of God, command that these stones be made bread." The key word in that statement was "if," in other words "prove it." Jesus wasn't going to do a "trick" to prove He is the Son of God. Then he (*Satan*) set Him up on a pinnacle of the temple and said to Him, "If thou be the Son of God, cast thyself down: for it is written, He shall give his angels charge concerning thee: and in their hands they shall bear thee up, lest at any time thou dash thy foot against a stone." (Don't be deceived, the devil knows the scriptures. He was quoting Psalm ninety one, verses eleven and twelve; "For He shall give His angels charge over thee, to keep thee in all thy ways. (V.12) They shall bear thee up in their hands, lest thou dash thy foot against a stone."). Jesus knowing this was true, came back with scripture Satan knew was true "Thou shalt not tempt the Lord thy God (*Deuteronomy 6:16*)." Jesus would die, but it was to be at the Fathers appointed time; and again; He didn't need to prove anything to Satan. If He had jumped He would be presuming His Father's power would protect Him. So, once again Jesus used the power of the scriptures as His answer.

Finally, the devil took Him up onto an exceeding high mountain, and showed Him all the kingdoms of the world, and the glory of them. And said to Him, "All these things will I give thee, if thou wilt fall down and worship me." The devil was trying to get Him to alienate His Father's honour, by giving it to him. "Then saith Jesus unto him, Get thee hence, Satan: for it is written, Thou shalt worship the Lord thy God, and Him only shalt thou serve." Jesus had had it with Satan and told him to go away.

Did you ever wonder why or how Satan was able to say "All these things will I give thee," to Jesus. Didn't they already belong to Jesus? The answer is yes and no. While God is ultimately in complete control of the universe, Corinthians 4:4 refers to Satan as "the god of this world." The reason he is called this goes back to Adam and Eve. God had given them dominion over all the earth. When they listened to the serpent (*Satan*), and ate of the forbidden fruit. They in a sense gave their dominion over the earth to the devil. This brings us back to the third temptation. Jesus being God knows all things. He knew when the time is right. Satan will be cast into the lake of fire, and God shall be all in all.

1 CORINTHIANS 15:24-28 - "Then cometh the end, when He shall have delivered up the kingdom to God, even the Father; when He shall have put down all rule and all authority and power.

(V.25) For He must reign, till He hath put all enemies under His feet. (V.26) The last enemy that shall be destroyed is death. (V.27) For He hath put all things under His feet. But when He saith all things are put under Him, it is manifest that He is excepted, which did put all things under Him. (V.28) And when all things shall be subdued unto Him, then shall the Son also Himself be subject unto Him that put all things under Him, that God may be all in all."

We have come to the last part of the temptation of Christ that is so important to us. When Jesus told Satan to go away, we see in verse eleven The words "Then the devil leaveth Him." James, the Brother of Jesus was inspired to give us these words of wisdom: "Submit yourselves therefore to God. Resist the devil, and he will flee from you (*James 4:7*)." Jesus endured and overcame the temptation by resisting the devil, and he left. *Just a note; Luke 4:13 says: "And when the devil had ended all the temptation, he departed from Him for a season."*

We read at the beginning of this chapter how Jesus was tempted in all points like we are. Why did God come to us in human form? To be our redeeming sacrifice for sin is true. However, He also needed to feel what we feel. He knows what it is like to be tempted. We can't say To Him "You don't understand what I'm going through." That's because He does. Think of some of the ways you are tempted, and then think about this, so was He.

HEBREWS 2:17 - "Wherefore in all things it behoved Him to be made like unto His brethren, that He might be a merciful and faithful high priest in things pertaining to God, to make reconciliation for the sins of the people. (V.18) For in that He Himself hath suffered being tempted, He is able to succour (*help*) them that are tempted."

JESUS AND WOMEN

When you picture Jesus out on the road with His followers. You probably have something like this in mind.

LUKE 8:1 - "And it came to pass afterward, that He went throughout every city and village, preaching and showing the glad tidings of the kingdom of God: and the twelve were with Him."

That would not be a correct picture. However, According to the next two verses, many women accompanied Jesus on His travels.

<u>**LUKE 8:2&3**</u> "And certain women, which had been healed of evil spirits and infirmities, <u>Mary called Magdalene</u>, out of whom went seven devils, (V.3) And <u>Joanna</u> the wife of Chuza Herod's steward, and <u>Susanna</u>, and <u>many others</u>, which ministered unto Him of their substance."

<u>**MARK 15:41**</u> - "(Who also, when He was in Galilee, followed Him, and ministered unto Him;) and <u>many other women</u> which came up with Him unto Jerusalem."

Who were these women, and what were they doing traveling with Jesus? I believe some of these others were; Mary the mother of James the less and of Joses (*John*), and Salome (*Mark 15:40*). We are told these women ministered unto Him, which basically means that they took care His needs (*cooked and served*). While some of the other women ministered unto Him out of their substance (*wealth*). In this chapter we will look at Jesus' dealings with women.

<u>MARY MAGDALENE</u>

In the life of Jesus He came in contact with many women named Mary. Of course the first one that comes to mind would have to be His mother. Another prominent one He had many dealings with is the mother of James and John; the wife of

Zebedee (*at times referred to as "the other Mary."*) She must have known Him well enough to make a selfish request for her sons. She was the one who went to Jesus and asked Him to "Grant that these my two sons may sit, the one on thy right hand, and the other on the left, in thy kingdom" (*Matthew 20:21*). There was also one of the sister of Lazarus. However, of all the Mary's Jesus knew, other than His mother, there was one (*Mary*) who was as special to Him, as He was to her; Mary Magdalene. We are introduced to her in the book of Luke.

LUKE 8:1&2 - "And it came to pass afterward, that He went throughout every city and village, preaching and showing the glad tidings of the kingdom of God: and the twelve were with Him, (V.2) And certain women, which had been healed of evil spirits and infirmities, Mary called Magdalene, out of whom went seven devils."

The Bible really doesn't give us much information about Mary Magdalene. We just know that she was possessed with seven devils that Jesus cast out. Next we will see a story that is debated of whether this was Mary Magdalene, or Mary the sister of Lazarus. Then we see her involvement on the morning of Jesus' resurrection. I'm sure she was in the upper room on the day of Pentecost; but there is no other mention of her after John 20:18.

LUKE 7:37&38 - "And, behold, a woman in

the city, which was a sinner, when she knew that Jesus sat at meat in the Pharisee's house, brought an alabaster box of ointment, (V.38) And stood at His feet behind Him weeping, and began to wash His feet with tears, and did wipe them with the hairs of her head, and kissed His feet, and anointed them with the ointment."

As I stated above, this event is under debate of which Mary the Bible is referring to. John 11:2 clearly tells us it was Mary the sister of Lazarus who did the anointing: ("It was that Mary which anointed the Lord with ointment, and wiped his feet with her hair, whose brother Lazarus was sick.") However, we will see that there two separate anointing that took place; one at Simon's house, and another at the house of Lazarus. We will look at the similarities and the differences to determine the outcome.

JOHN 12:1 - "Then Jesus six days before the Passover came to Bethany, where Lazarus was which had been dead, whom he raised from the dead. (V.2) There they made Him a supper; and Martha served: but Lazarus was one of them that sat at the table with Him."

In the first scripture on this topic we see this anointing being done at a Pharisee's house. Matthew, Mark and Luke tell the story of it being at a man named Simon's house. Mark 14:3: "And being in Bethany in the house of Simon the leper, as He sat at meat, there came a woman having an alabaster box of ointment of spikenard very precious; and she brake the box, and poured it on His head." Notice here it said that she poured it on His head. In John it tells us this woman "anointed the feet of Jesus."

It may seem like some small things to mention, but John goes on to mention that "Lazarus was one of them that sat at the table with Him" Why would He be mentioned if it wasn't his house? What would Lazarus be doing at the house of Simon the leper?

Another thing was that Simon desired Jesus to eat with him (*Luke 7:36*). In John it appears that Jesus was in Bethany. When He was there it was His custom to eat at the house of Lazarus, Martha and Mary, and "There they made Him a supper."

Something written in Luke 7:50 is quite compelling. After the woman was done anointing Jesus. He told her "Thy faith hath saved thee; go in peace." If this was Mary the sister of Lazarus, why would He tell her to leave her own house?

I noticed an interesting occurrence in the anointing itself. Matthew and Mark state that the ointment was poured on the head of Jesus, nothing more. Luke and John add a little more to the story in their writings.

LUKE7:38 - "And stood at His feet behind Him weeping, and began to wash His feet with tears, and did wipe them with the hairs of her head, and kissed His feet, and anointed them with the ointment."

<u>JOHN 12:3</u> - "Then took Mary a pound of ointment of spikenard, very costly, and anointed the feet of Jesus, and wiped His feet with her hair: and the house was filled with the odour of the ointment."

I want you to look real closely to the details in each story. Luke's account involves a repentant sinner woman (*who was not Mary Magdalene*). She washes feet with tears. In John's account, Mary, the sister of Lazarus, sheds no tears. Luke tells us that she "kissed His feet." Not so with Mary. She only anointed His feet, and wiped His feet with her hair. Which brings back to John 11:2: "It was that Mary which anointed the Lord with ointment, and wiped his feet with her hair, whose brother Lazarus was sick."

However, there are a few things you can't overlook. In every instance the woman is berated for wasting the costly ointment, and how it could have been sold for much, and given to the poor. Mark and John both mention three hundred pence as a price.

In three Gospels (*all but Luke*), Jesus states "the poor always ye have with you."

The one statement that really makes this look like one instance is found in Mark and John. Both say that she was anointing Him for His burial.

MARK 14:8 - "She hath done what she could: she is come aforehand to anoint my body to the burying."

JOHN 12:7 - "Then said Jesus, Let her alone: against the day of my burying hath she kept this."

Matthew and Mark and add a very profound ending at the close of their account of this story. In both Jesus says to those present, "I say unto you, Wheresoever this gospel shall be preached in the whole world, there shall also this, that this woman hath done, be told for a memorial of her (*Matthew 26:13*)." Luke, even though it's the same account, does not mention it. Neither does John. However, John does not mention some things the other Gospels do, and does mention things they don't. This is why John 11:2: "It was that Mary which anointed the Lord with ointment, and wiped his feet with her hair, whose brother Lazarus was sick," brings up this very topic. She is found anointing His feet in Chapter Twelve. I know it is not worded this way, but many think it was referring to what she would do. John does not mention the account at Simon's house.

John12:1 requires a little reading between the lines, but there is no doubt this was done at Lazarus, Martha, and Mary's house. Why would

Martha be serving at Simon's house? Now granted, both were done in Bethany. However I do not see Mary doing the same thing twice, and at different locations. We need to also note that in Luke's account the woman was known as a sinner. This could have been anyone, but most scholars believe it was not Mary Magdalene. The only reason for thinking it was her is because of John 11:2 saying it was Mary that anointed Jesus. They just assumed that it was Mary Magdalene, because of her past. Another difference that may seem small but was a big deal back then was the kissing of Jesus' feet. Luke mentions it in his account; John does not.

<u>JOHN 12:3</u> - "Then took Mary a pound of ointment of spikenard, very costly, and anointed the feet of Jesus, and wiped His feet with her hair: and the house was filled with the odour of the ointment."

As I said it may not seem like a big deal today. But this woman kissing the feet of Jesus was something to be noted. Especially after what the Pharisee said in Luke 7:39: "This man, if He were a prophet, would have known who and what manner of woman this is that toucheth Him: for she is a sinner.

The "kicker" if you want to call it is the timeline. In Mathew we are told the anointing at Simon the lepers house was two days before the Passover. In John's account we are told it took place six days before the Passover.

I and many others believe these are two separate events. Yes, Mary Lazarus's sister did anoint Jesus at her house, not at Simons.

The last time we read of Mary Magdalene is on resurrection morning. Interesting enough, every one of the four gospels mentions her by name as one of the women who came to the sepulchre on that glorious day.

JOHN 20:1&2, 11-18 - "The first day of the week cometh Mary Magdalene early, when it was yet dark, unto the sepulchre, and seeth the stone taken away from the sepulchre. (V.2) Then she runneth, and cometh to Simon Peter, and to the other disciple, whom Jesus loved, and saith unto them, They have taken away the Lord out of the sepulchre, and we know not where they have laid Him.

(V.11) But Mary stood without at the sepulchre weeping: and as she wept, she stooped down, and looked into the sepulchre, (V.12) And seeth two angels in white sitting, the one at the head, and the other at the feet, where the body of Jesus had lain. (V.13) And they say unto her, Woman, why weepest thou? She saith unto them, Because they have taken away my Lord, and I know not where they have laid Him. (V.14) And when she had thus said, she turned herself back, and saw Jesus standing, and knew not that it was Jesus. (V.15) Jesus saith unto her, Woman, why weepest thou?

whom seekest thou? She, supposing Him to be the gardener, saith unto Him, Sir, if thou have borne Him hence, tell me where thou hast laid Him, and I will take Him away. (V.16) Jesus saith unto her, Mary. She turned herself, and saith unto Him, Rabboni; which is to say, Master. (V.17) Jesus saith unto her, Touch me not; for I am not yet ascended to my Father: but go to my brethren, and say unto them, I ascend unto my Father, and your Father; and to my God, and your God. (V.18) Mary Magdalene came and told the disciples that she had seen the Lord, and that He had spoken these things unto her."

At the start of this chapter I said there was one (*Mary*) who was as special to Jesus, as He was to her. Are you wondering what did I mean by that? In the scripture section above is where we find the answer.

In verse eighteen we see that Mary had seen the risen savior. Mark 16:9: "Now when Jesus was risen early the first day of the week, He appeared first to Mary Magdalene, out of whom He had cast seven devils." This was a requirement for apostleship. In verse seventeen, Mary was granted the honor to be the first person to go proclaim that He had indeed risen from the dead.

There is a debated yet interesting point found in verse seventeen. Jesus told Mary "Touch me not." Yet In the same chapter we see Him telling Thomas "Reach hither thy finger, and behold my hands; and reach hither thy hand, and thrust it into my side (V.27)." This is not a contradiction. The word He spoke to Mary was "Haptomai", which means to fasten one's self to, adhere to, or cling to. The word He spoke to Thomas was "Eido" which means to perceive by any of the senses, inspect, and examine. Mary wanted to cling to Jesus and not let Him leave her again. On the other hand He wanted Thomas to know it was really Him.

As I said before, the Bible does not give us much information on her; so now the time has come to leave the study of Mary Magdalene. Although, I feel that I make one last point clear. Jesus and Mary Magdalene were never married. You may feel that is obvious. Yet you would not believe how many people think that they were.

There are a few more women that came into the life of Jesus I think are worth mentioning.

First, is His Mother Mary. As I told you earlier. While He was on the cross. One of the last things did was to make sure she was going to be taken care of after He was gone.

JOHN 19:26&27 - "When Jesus therefore saw His mother, and the disciple standing by, whom He loved (*John*), He saith unto his mother, Woman, behold thy son!(V.27) Then saith He to the disciple, Behold thy mother! And from that hour that disciple took her unto his own home."

That was His loving Mother. However He also

met the needs of some women with "questionable" reputations.

There was a Samaritan woman He met at Jacob's well (*John 4:5-30*). The fact that she was there about the sixth hour (*12 noon*), probably meant the other women of the city wouldn't associate with her when they went for water at an earlier hour. Jesus knew all about her sinful life but didn't condemn her. She is one of the few people Jesus told that He was the Messiah!

JOHN 4:25&26 - "The woman saith unto him, I know that Messias cometh, which is called Christ: when He is come, He will tell us all things.

(V.26) Jesus saith unto her, <u>I that speak unto thee am He</u>.

This encounter ended with her going into the city and telling them "Come, see a man, which told me all things that ever I did: is not this the Christ?" (*John 4:29*) I believe she believed.

Then later while He was teaching. (*John 8:3-11*) He was confronted by the scribes and Pharisees with a woman taken in adultery (*the very act*). This is the classic story where we hear Jesus say "He that is without sin among you, let him first cast a stone at her." Of course they all dropped their rocks and left. The story ends like this

JOHN 8:10&11 - "When Jesus had lifted up Himself, and saw none but the woman, He said unto her, Woman, where are those thine accusers? hath no man condemned thee? (V.11) She said, No man, Lord. And Jesus said unto her, <u>Neither do I</u> condemn thee: go, and sin no more."

As I said above, He met the needs of these women. I greatest need we have is forgiveness.
I'm sure there were other women in the life of Jesus. However, the Scriptures don't mention them, so neither will I.

<u>WHAT IS JESUS DOING NOW?</u>

You may be saying "that was then, this is now." What is Jesus doing today? Jesus is keeping very busy helping us, because we can't help ourselves. Hebrews 7:25 says that "He ever liveth to make intercession" for us. In the verses below we will see some of those ways He is helping us on a daily basis. With Him being our intercessor, our advocate, and our mediator.

<u>**ROMANS 8:26 &27**</u> - "Likewise the Spirit also helpeth our infirmities: for we know not what we should pray for as we ought: but the Spirit itself

maketh intercession for us with groanings which cannot be uttered. (V.27) And He that searcheth the hearts knoweth what is the mind of the Spirit, because He maketh intercession for the saints according to the will of God."

ROMANS 8:34 - "Who is he that condemneth? It is Christ that died, yea rather, that is risen again, who is even at the right hand of God, who also maketh intercession for us."

HEBREWS 7:25 - "Wherefore He is able also to save them to the uttermost that come unto God by Him, seeing He ever liveth to make intercession for them."

An intercessor goes to or meets with a person, especially for the purpose of conversation, consultation, or supplication. Indeed, Jesus is seated at the right hand of God. However He still goes to God on our behalf.

1 JOHN 2:1 - "My little children, these things write I unto you, that ye sin not. And if any man sin, we have an advocate with the Father, Jesus Christ the righteous."

An advocate is one who pleads another's cause before a judge, a pleader, also called a counsel for defense. Jesus placed at God's right hand, is our advocate is pleading our case with God the Father for the pardon of our sins.

1 TIMOTHY 2:5 - "For there is one God, and one mediator between God and men, the man Christ Jesus."

A mediator is one who intervenes between two, either in order to make or restore peace and friendship, or form a compact, or for ratifying a covenant. Jesus as our intercessor and advocate to God helps bring harmony back into the relationship we have with Him. God loves us no matter what, but that doesn't mean He's always pleased with our actions. I have no scripture for this but when we sin I feel Jesus shows God the nail prints in His hands, and says I did this for them. Therefore He is the only one who can restore peace between us and God the Father.

ROMANS 5:1 - "Therefore being justified by faith, we have peace with God through our Lord Jesus Christ."

There is another thing Jesus is doing for us. I'll let the scripture speak for itself.

JOHN 14:2&3 - "In my Father's house are many mansions: if it were not so, I would have told you. I go to prepare a place for you. (V.3) And if I go and prepare a place for you, I will come again, and receive you unto myself; that where I am, there ye may be also."

I know that God spoke the world into existence in six days. Jesus has been gone almost two thousand years now. Don't you think He'd be done "preparing a place" for us by now? I don't know. We need to recall 1 Corinthians 2:9 where Paul wrote by revelation; "But as it is written, Eye hath not seen, nor ear heard, neither have entered into the heart of man, the things which God hath prepared for them that love Him. Not that it would be a time consuming thing for Him to do; but it must be some kind of a wonderful place.

<u>ENCORE</u>

I use the word "encore" for this chapter because of the meaning of the word. It means an extra or repeated performance. Jesus will come back to Earth some day. We just saw that He is not sitting around waiting for that day to come. He is still saving the lost, healing the sick, delivering the oppressed, and must more that He "preformed" while He was here on earth.

We agree that Jesus was born, He died, He was buried, He rose from the dead, and He ascended to heaven where He is sitting at the right hand of God?

<u>1 CORINTHIANS 15:3&4</u> - "For I delivered unto you first of all that which I also received, how that Christ died for our sins according to the scriptures; (V.4) And that He was buried, and that He rose again the third day according to the scriptures."

<u>HEBREWS 12:2</u> - "Looking unto Jesus the author and finisher of our faith; who for the joy that was set before Him endured the cross, despising the shame, and is set down at the right hand of the throne of God."

"According to the scriptures," Jesus is sitting at the right hand of God. He will not be seen again until He comes for His bride (*the church*) in the rapture. When will this be? No one knows not even Jesus Himself (*Matthew 24:36: "But of that day and hour knoweth no man, no, not the angels of heaven, but my Father only"*).

<u>1 THESSALONIANS 4:16&17</u> -"For the Lord Himself shall descend from heaven with a shout, with the voice of the archangel, and with the trump of God: and the dead in Christ shall rise first: (V.17) Then we which are alive and remain shall be caught up together with them in the clouds, to meet the Lord in the air: and so shall we ever be with the Lord."

Did you raise an eyebrow, or scratch your head when I said "He will not be seen again until He comes for His bride (the church) in the rapture?" If you know your bible, you should have. Are you aware that Jesus was seen by men after He ascended to heaven? The Apostle Paul was one of these men. A note about Paul; I just wanted to let you know that God did not change Sauls' name to Paul. Acts 13:9 says "Then Saul, (who also is called Paul)." People knew Saul was a persecutor of Christians. So he took on the name Paul .We begin his story with him being a persecutor of Christians. Acts 9:1and 2 tell us that he (*Saul / Paul*) went to the high priest, "And desired of him letters to Damascus to the synagogues, that if he found any of this way, whether they were men or women, he might bring them bound unto Jerusalem." The following is an account of what happened on that journey.

<u>ACTS 9:3-8</u> - "And as he (*Saul*) journeyed, he came near Damascus: and suddenly there shined round about him a light from heaven: (V.4) And he fell to the earth, and heard a voice saying unto him, Saul, Saul, why persecutest thou me? (V.5) And he said, Who art thou, Lord? And the Lord said, I am Jesus whom thou persecutest: it is hard for thee to kick against the pricks. (V.6) And he trembling and astonished said, Lord, what wilt thou have me to do? And the Lord said unto him, Arise, and go into the city, and it shall be told thee what thou must do. (V.7) And the men which journeyed with him stood speechless, hearing a voice, but seeing no man. (V.8) And Saul arose from the earth; and when his eyes were opened, he saw no man: but they led him by the hand, and brought him into Damascus."

There is no doubt that Saul had an encounter with Jesus. This is made clear in verse five where Saul asked "Who art thou, Lord?" And he got the answer of, "I am Jesus whom thou persecutest." Now, the question must be asked; did Saul see Jesus or just a light? The men that journeyed with him heard a voice, but saw no man. This is where reading your whole bible is essential. Paul gives the answer to us and the Corinthians in his first letter to them.

1 CORINTHIANS 15:4-9 - "And that He was buried, and that He rose again the third day according to the scriptures: (V.5) And that He was seen of Cephas, then of the twelve: (V.6) After that, He was seen of above five hundred brethren at once; of whom the greater part remain unto this present, but some are fallen asleep. (V.7) After that, He was seen of James; then of all the apostles. (V.8) And last of all He was seen of me also, as of one born out of due time. (V.9) For I am the least of the apostles, that am not meet to be called an apostle, because I persecuted the church of God."

There was a situation where Paul had to defend his position as an Apostle to the Corinthians. It was a requirement of an apostle to be a witness of Jesus' resurrection*. Back in 1Corinthians 9:1Paul asked them; "Am I not an apostle? am I not free? have I not seen Jesus Christ our Lord? are not ye my work in the Lord?"
* Let's go back to the vacancy made by the death of Judas. The sin of Judas was not only his shame and ruin, but it made a vacancy in the group of the apostles. There were twelve selected and now they needed to fill up the vacancy.

ACTS 1:16 & 17 - "Men and brethren, this scripture must needs have been fulfilled, which the Holy Ghost by the mouth of David spake before concerning Judas, which was guide to them that took Jesus. (V.17) For he was numbered with us, and had obtained part of this ministry."

PSALM 109:8 -"Let his days be few; and let another take his office."

But who and how should this replacement be appointed? Jesus selected the first twelve. Interestingly enough, Jesus knew who he was picking (John 6:70 &71: "Jesus answered them, Have not I chosen you twelve, and one of you is a devil? (V.71) He spake of Judas Iscariot the son of

Simon: for he it was that should betray Him, being one of the twelve.")

He must be a witness of Jesus' resurrection. But by this, the apostles could not have been witnesses of his resurrection. The very thing which the apostles were to tell the world was about Christ's resurrection, for this was the proof of His being the Messiah.

ACTS 1:21&22 - "Wherefore of these men which have companied with us all the time that the Lord Jesus went in and out among us, (V.22) Beginning from the baptism of John, unto that same day that he was taken up from us, must one be ordained to be a witness with us of His resurrection."

So, if you are still wondering; yes, Saul saw the risen savior that day on the road to Damascus. This was his proof that he was indeed also an apostle.

The other person who saw Jesus after He a ascended to heaven was the Apostle John. After previous unsuccessful attempts to silence John, he was exiled to the island of Patmos, left to die there.

REVELATION 1:9 - "I John, who also am your brother, and companion in tribulation, and in the kingdom and patience of Jesus Christ, was in the isle that is called Patmos, for the word of God, and for the testimony of Jesus Christ."

You will notice this section of scripture starts with "I was in the Spirit." I need to note that this was a real event happening in the flesh, not some mystical spirit world. I personally have been "in the Spirit" many times and never left my body. I'm mentioning this to silence the critics who will no doubt say John was just dreaming this. I believe John actually saw Jesus as He is now.

REVELATION 1:10-18 - "I was in the Spirit on the Lord's day, and heard behind me a great voice, as of a trumpet, (V.11) Saying, I am Alpha and Omega, the first and the last: and, What thou seest, write in a book, and send it unto the seven churches which are in Asia; unto Ephesus, and unto Smyrna, and unto Pergamos, and unto Thyatira, and unto Sardis, and unto Philadelphia, and unto Laodicea. (V.12) And I turned to see the voice that spake with me. And being turned, I saw seven golden candlesticks; (V.13) And in the midst of the seven candlesticks one like unto the Son of man, clothed with a garment down to the foot, and girt about the paps with a golden girdle. (V.14) His head and His hairs were white like wool, as white as snow; and His eyes were as a flame of fire; (V.15) And His feet like unto fine brass, as if they burned in a furnace; and His voice as the sound of many waters. (V.16) And He had in his right hand seven stars: and out of His mouth went a sharp twoedged sword: and His countenance was as the sun shineth in His strength. (V.17) And when I saw Him, I fell at his feet * as dead. And He laid his right hand upon me, saying unto me, Fear not; I am the first and the last: (V.18) I am He that liveth, and was dead; and, behold, I am alive for evermore, Amen; and have the keys of hell and of death."

A note as to why the phrase "I fell at his feet" is so important; "worship God."

REVELATION 19:9 &10 - "And he saith unto me, Write, Blessed are they which are called unto the marriage supper of the Lamb. And he saith unto me, These are the true sayings of God. Revelation (V.10) And <u>I fell at his feet to worship him</u>. And he said unto me, See thou do it not: I am thy fellowservant, and of thy brethren that have the testimony of Jesus: **worship God**: for the testimony of Jesus is the spirit of prophecy."

* **REVELATION 22:8&9** - "And I John saw these things, and heard them. And when I had heard and seen, <u>I fell down to worship before the feet of the angel</u> which showed me these things. (V.9) Then saith he unto me, <u>See thou do it not</u>: for I am thy fellowservant, and of thy brethren the prophets, and of them which keep the sayings of this book: **worship God**."

There are two more men that need to be mentioned, Stephen and Ananias (*not the Ananias, with his wife Sapphira*). After Stephen had given the Jews a history lesson. He was actually being chewed on before he was stoned to death. Acts 7:54: "When they heard these things, they were cut to the heart, and they gnashed on him with their teeth." Acts 7:59; "And they stoned Stephen, calling upon God, and saying, Lord Jesus, receive my spirit." Knowing he was going to die, He looked to Jesus his Savior.

ACTS 7:55, 56, 59 - "But he (Stephen), being full of the Holy Ghost, looked up stedfastly into heaven, and saw the glory of God, and Jesus standing on the right hand of God, (V.56) And said, Behold, I see the heavens opened, and the Son of man standing on the right hand of God. (V.59) And they stoned Stephen, calling upon God, and saying, Lord Jesus, receive my spirit."

It has been mentioned several times in this chapter that Jesus is sitting at the right hand of God. However, did you notice Stephen said he saw Jesus "standing on the right hand of God." This is not a contradiction of the word. I do believe Jesus is sitting at the right hand of God. But what's not to mention that He could have stood up to welcome Stephen home.

Where Stephen actually saw Jesus; Ananias saw "the Lord in a vision." But who is to say this vision wasn't the Lord Himself?

<u>ACTS 9:10-12</u> - "And there was a certain disciple at Damascus, named Ananias; and to him said the Lord in a vision, Ananias. And he said, Behold, I am here, Lord. (V.11) And the Lord said unto him, Arise, and go into the street which is called Straight, and inquire in the house of Judas for one called Saul, of Tarsus: for, behold, he prayeth, (V.12) And hath seen in a vision a man named Ananias coming in, and putting his hand on him, that he might receive his sight."

You might have noticed that Saul also had a vision, which might discount the vision Ananias had. I don't believe that is so. The Greek word used for vision is "Horama." This word has two meanings (*which isn't uncommon*); one is "that which is seen," and the other is "a sight divinely granted in an ecstasy or in a sleep." So, while Ananias certainly could have seen Jesus (*after all he did have a conversation with Him*). Saul (*who was blind at this time*) certainly could not have seen Jesus except for a divine intervention while praying.

The whole purpose of this chapter is to show that Jesus is alive forevermore. He is not just sitting up in heaven waiting on His Father to tell Him it's time to go receive His bride (the church) in the rapture. He is actively engaging in the life of those who have put their trust in Him.

When He ascended up to heaven, it was the

end of the "show" for Him. He came out and did some "encores!"

JOHN 20:30 &31 - *"And many other signs truly did Jesus in the presence of His disciples, which are not written in this book: (V.31) But these are written, that ye might believe that Jesus is the Christ, the Son of God; and that believing ye might have life through His name."*

NOTES